Gray-Haired
Grins & Giggles

Enjoy!

Margaret G. Bigger

Gray-Haired Grins & Giggles

Guess What - Grammy & Grandy Have a Sense of Humor, Too!

160 stories from 45 authors

Edited by
Margaret G. Bigger

Illustrated by
Loyd Dillon

ABB   A. Borough Books   Charlotte NC

ISBN 0-9640606-3-9

Library of Congress Catalog Card Number 95-77859

Printed in the United States of America

ABB

A. Borough Books
P.O. Box 15391
Charlotte NC 28211

INTRODUCTION

What sets senior humor apart from "junior" humor?

Good question! Two seasoned citizens reading the same story will react---and repeat it---differently. But then, whatever your age, you and your best friend will, too!

Humor is subjective. What one person thinks is hilarious may sound disgusting to someone else. A punchline that causes a chuckle from a demure Southern socialite evokes guffaws from the Midwesterner in a red plaid shirt sitting across the aisle.

If you don't believe this, make several photocopies of a page of short anecdotal humor from a magazine. On one of them, mark in the margin beside each story an L (laughed out loud), S (smiled), N (neutral: "Someone else might think this is funny, but not I!") or C (cull this out: "Who could possibly have seen humor in this?"). Give the other copies to a friend from another part of the country, a neighbor of the opposite sex, an acquaintance of a different socio-economic group, a teenager, your grandfather and people of various backgrounds. Ask them to make the same notations. You will find, as many of these authors and I did, that an anecdote which has a bold L on your sheet will have an emphatic C on someone else's.

People bring their own personal experiences to a story and judge it accordingly. We did, however, determine some generalities about humor preferences that the majority of us senior citizens could agree on. On the other hand, we do not like putdowns or insulting jests. Four-letter words and filth are "turn offs." Explicit sex is "out." Cursing is uncouth and unnecessary. You'll find none of this in our book.

Instead, as we laugh *at* ourselves and *with* others who have crossed our paths, and while we're looking at life through crinkled eyes, you'll discover something about us---and yourself.

Do we expect all Ls? Of course, not. But if you hit a few Ns or Cs, read on. We're hoping for your grins and giggles, but we'll settle for some gentle smiles.

AUTHORS
WHERE TO FIND THEIR STORIES

Contents

NO KIDDING, WE WERE KIDS ONCE

The Seventh Commandment

My mother never lied to us about anything except Santa Claus, the Easter bunny and where babies came from. I believed everything she said. After all, I almost always got what I wanted on Christmas mornings and a basket of colored eggs every Easter. Storks, on three occasions, had brought me baby brothers during the night.

When I was about 10 years old (in the early 1930s), I attended First Methodist Church in Clarksdale, Mississippi. One of my Sunday school assignments was to memorize the Ten Commandments.

Mother was quite busy in the kitchen, so I took my Bible in there and sat at the table reciting out loud. The first six commandments I knew very well. However, when I got to the seventh, "Thou shalt not commit adultery," suddenly I realized I didn't know what that meant. It had not been explained by the Sunday school teacher, nor had I ever heard that word at my home.

"Mother, what's adultery?" I asked.

My mother's arms stiffened in the sink. A quick thinker, she replied without any hesitation at all. "That's sticking your tongue out at your neighbor."

I was horrified---I had committed adultery with my brothers! When I became angry, I'd stick out my tongue at them and make a "face." I vowed never to do that at my brothers or friends again.

Thereafter, I was appalled when I saw my playmates settle a fuss by sticking out their tongues at their opponents. I'd think, "Oh, no! They've committed adultery! They broke one of the Ten Commandments. How terrible!"

I was 20 years old when I found out that Mother had lied to me.

- Martha Patterson Spille Hendren

9

Once the Baby, Always the Baby!

When asked by her first grade teacher about whether the new sibling in the house was a "pretty baby," my sister honestly replied. "No, but we THINK she's gonna be."

Imagine my lifelong chagrin at having endured the following chorus at each family reunion: "We're still *way-ay-ting*."

- Sally DePriest

Child of the '40s

My parents always had a rationale for the birth of each child. My brother was the "Depression" baby, my sister was the "Goodtimes" baby, and I was the "Sugar" baby. Why "Sugar" baby? Because my World War II birth enabled the growing family to qualify for another much-needed sugar ration book!

- Sally DePriest

Madness

At about the age of 10, my playmate, Ginny, and I sometimes got mad at one another. Our parents were friends because our dads were both lawyers in Worcester, Massachusetts. In our spats, it was not unusual for one of us to taunt, "Your father's a liar; *my* father's a lawyer!"

- Harriet Dolin

Wow!

During a Sunday school picnic in Pike County, Georgia, my mother was sitting on the bleachers with the crowd to watch the swimmers. It was during the late 'teens, the first year girls were swimming without hose and had one-piece bathing suits. I was about 14 years old.

In my rush to get to the pool, I scrambled up and out on the diving board. Mother cringed when a woman several rows back exclaimed, "My gosh, look! I was married to John *ten years* before he saw that much of me!"

- Janie Hardy

10

What's So Funny?

On Sunday afternoons in the mid-'20s, our family would pile into the trusty old Chevy and set out for the Ohio countryside, singing lustily all the way. My stepfather Earle had been "over there" in World War I, and he would belt out that song as well as "Yankee Doodle Dandy" and "Lili Marlene." We'd let him do some solos, then we would join in for other numbers.

One day, after about exhausting our repertoire, Earle asked, "Are there any more we haven't done yet?"

"I know! Sing the one about the rubbers!" I said.

Well, the folks burst out in guffaws, totally convulsed.

I was indignant! "What's so funny?" I wanted to know, but they wouldn't tell me. It was a silly little ditty about the farmer and his wife and their trip to the county fair, with a lilting tune and catchy words, but not *that* hilarious.

Years passed before I finally discovered the reason for their reaction. Still, Earle could not resist asking me occasionally, "Do you want to hear the one about the rubbers?"

The last two lines of the chorus which did me in were:

"Well, I swan, I must be gettin' on.

"Drap around to see me, when your overshoes are gone."

- Margaret Bates

Grandma's Oil Lamp

Before electricity came to our farm in North Carolina, my sister Betsy and I used Grandma's old kerosene lamp with a brass bottom and a fancy glass globe for lighting in our room, and we loved it. There seemed to be something magical about Grandma's lamp, because we discovered, if you held it a certain way, your face appeared beautiful.

Betsy, who was 16, was expecting her first date, and I, at 13, was envying her, when we decided to practice the technique of presenting Betsy in the best possible light. Again and again, my vain, determined sister entered the room, and finally I found the perfect angle for Grandma's lamp to transform Betsy's face. Of course, we were intrigued, as well, with the resemblance of the bride walking down the aisle to her future husband, holding her bouquet.

When the night of Betsy's first date arrived, I greeted Norman, the shy young man at the door, invited him in then excused myself as instructed.

As Betsy made her grand entrance, holding Grandma's lamp and looking especially lovely, I couldn't help but think of the many times I had pleaded with Betsy to let me hold the lamp, so she could make my face beautiful, but she had refused.

The teenage boy must have wondered what he was getting himself into, when as Betsy made her entrance, he heard from the adjoining room my sing-song voice, "Here comes the bride."

- Lexie Hill

Umm, Umm, Good!

One summer in the 1920s, my father Fenner, his brother Hugh and sister Ella rented a large house on the island of Ocracoke, North Carolina, for a multi-generational gathering. With so many of us children, all ages, they had a rule that anyone who complained about the food had to wash the dishes.

Someone stuck a big chunk of soap on the back of Uncle Hugh's soup spoon, and when he began his meal, he said, "This soup tastes like soap!" He hesitated a minute and added, "But it's good!"

- Marjorie Phillips Carson

Testing, Testing

The first telephone that we had at our home in Washington, North Carolina, was installed in the early '20s. Our number was 551, and the phone hung on the wall in our downstairs back hall. It was so high that we young children had to stand on a stool to reach it.

One day when the phone rang, my mother answered it. Someone on the line said, "I'm testing your telephone. Stand to the left of the phone and say, 'hello.'"

Mother did.

Then the person said, "Stand to the right and say 'hello,'" so she did.

Then she was asked to stand on her head and say "hello."

Of course, it was a very long time before she lived that one down.

- Marjorie Phillips Carson

Picking on Poor Miss Brown

Miss Brown, our sixth grade teacher was having us take turns reading our geography lesson aloud.

Of course, all of us were carefully following the reader in our oversize books. Mine was identical to the rest with one significant difference. The opportunity was too good to miss. I propped my book in front of me on the desk, so that Miss Brown could not help but notice that the title was upside down.

Notice she did, and she drew the obvious but incorrect conclusion: James has his book upside down and is busy doing something he shouldn't be doing behind the big geography book!

She did not get up and walk around her huge teacher's desk. Oh no! With a show of inspired strength, she threw the desk to one side, dashed down the aisle to my desk and snatched up my book to expose whatever mischief James was up to!

Imagine her bitter disappointment and embarrassment when she discovered that the section of my book we were reading was printed upside down.

- Jim Shearouse

Shasta

When I turned 16 and wanted to learn to drive a car, Daddy said a great big "NO!" I'm sure he was concerned for my safety, and his answer when I brought up the subject was always, "When I'm ready to bury you, I'll give you a car and teach you to drive."

Drivers licenses were not required until the late 1930s, and so all you needed was access to a car and permission to drive it from your parents. Mama, who had never learned to drive, needed a chauffeur, and when I turned 18, Daddy finally relented.

My cousin, Jim Rawlings came over to see the little black 1934 Chevrolet sedan. "What are you going to name it?" he asked.

"Name it? What kind of name could be given to a car?"

"Shasta," he said. "You know, shasta have gas, shasta have oil, shasta have tires."

So, Shasta she was. Shasta take Mama, shasta take me, shasta show off sometimes, too.

- Catherine Todd McSwain

Never Talk to Strangers

The year was 1948, and as I settled into my train berth for my first trip home from boarding school, I was vociferously showing off my newly-acquired "sophisticated" vocabulary to impress the classmates traveling in the same sleeping car. Every other word was "damn" or "hell."

At length, the curtains of the opposite berth parted, and a dignified man poked his head through the opening. Peering over his glasses, he asked, "Did one of you say you were from Spartanburg? What is your name, my dear?"

With an impudent toss of my 16-year-old curls, I retorted, "*My* name's Bet Shepherd. What's *yours*?"

"I'm Dr. Ward," said the head ever so gently. "I do believe I'm your new pastor."

- Bet Ancrum

Here Comes the Bride!

My mother was a romantic. She, my big brother and I lived in Del Rio, Texas, during World War I, when my father was an Army captain in the United States Cavalry.

Mother's romantic mind was never at a loss. When time began to hang heavy, she decided to dress me up like a bride with veil, bouquet and train and marry me off to Frank Taylor Hyde, a 4-year-old boy from Charleston, South Carolina. (Frank was so enamored of 3-year-old me that he had kissed me in the grocery store.) My brother, Rob, was the preacher and Frank's brother, Tris, was the best man. She took a picture of the wedding.

When I was about 20, I went to a debutante party in Richmond, Virginia. My visit was reported in the Richmond paper.

As I was dancing, suddenly I heard a deep voice at my elbow. "Great God, it's my wife!"

Of course, it was Frank Taylor. We dated, and it was probably the dullest date either of us ever had.

But Mother was thrilled.

- Katherine Kennedy McIntyre

YoYo

In 1919, our family lived in Camden, South Carolina, a small Southern town. Private schools were popular then. It was in such a school that my brother, Rob, began his education.

At the end of the first week, he came home and announced proudly, "I was at the head of my class this week."

Our parents congratulated him.

After his second week, he reported sadly, "I was at the bottom of my class this week."

At the end of the third week, he came home smiling. "I was at the head of my class this week."

Our father asked, "Rob, who is in your class?"

"Me and Margaret."

- Katherine Kennedy McIntyre

How DO You Do?

When I was in the 9th grade in Camden, South Carolina, my brother, Rob, invited me to a dance at The Citadel in Charleston.

I was all excited---but intimidated---by the thought of meeting Rob's important college friends.

Before the dance, Rob took me to Folly Beach for a swim in the ocean. I headed for the beach house to change into my new lavender bathing suit. Up the steps I went. I opened the first door I saw inside.

There before me was a stark naked man as big as a mountain. He stared at me. I stared at him before murmuring, "Excuse me" and fleeing.

Twenty minutes later, my brother introduced me to 6'3" Ed from Lancaster, South Carolina.

Ed smiled, "We've already met."

- Katherine Kennedy McIntyre

Some News Unfit to Print

When Charlotte was a much smaller place, some of us staffers of Central High's literary magazine (called *Lace and Pig Iron*, if you must know) found another outlet for our creativity. We girls invented a lady, named her Ruby Knox and gave her a hometown, Troutman.

From then on, the fun was to see how many notices we could place in "The Social Scene," a column in the Society section of *The Charlotte News*. Ruby frequently visited Charlotte, sometimes for two weeks at a time. She was feted at Buffet Luncheons and Morning Coca-Colas.

For the climax of Ruby's adventures, she appeared in the flesh, courtesy of one of the tricksters. Caroline Weeks offered her home for an Afternoon Tea at which the elusive Miss Knox was to be honored.

The Social Scene obediently prophesied the event. The senior writers gathered at the Weeks home; some attempted disguises such as dying red hair gray with Golden Glint rinse. Caroline's mother, innocent of the farce, seated herself behind the silver teapot in the dining room. Suppressed hilarity filled the room.

Laughter broke out when Ruby arrived. In a failed effort at nonchalance, she entered smirking and looking a lot like one of the staff---Suzanne in her first black dress.

Puzzled and tight-lipped, Mrs. Weeks bravely filled everyone's teacup. But when the inspired writers had happily eaten all the little sandwiches and cakes she had provided and Ruby Knox was departing, she turned to the rest of her guests and said disdainfully, "You can always tell when somebody has a new dress."

- Nancy West

The Permanent Wave

Hair styles have always been important to us girls, and I was no exception. I was fortunate enough to have been born a blond with hair not too difficult to manage. As a young teenager in the late '30s, I sometimes received compliments on my hair which, I'm sure, went straight to my head (pun intended).

A permanent wave, as we called them then, seemed to be the answer to all that nightly rolling and fuss to look really swell the next day. Finally, my mother agreed to it and hauled me off to the upstairs beauty parlor in downtown Raleigh. I was *so* excited, I could hardly wait.

When my turn came to be "fixed," I sat down in the leather-bound beauty chair and anxiously waited for the beautician to work her magic. First came the wash, then the rollers through which the heat would be circulated. Above my head was the huge machine from which hung many little contraptions suspended from wires, a giant octopus with far too many tentacles. In retrospect, I'm not sure but what a sea creature couldn't have done a better job with my locks.

Once attached to the monster above my head, I resembled the mythological Medusa. Then the contraption was plugged in, and the heat began to flow. The smell was horrendous when heat hit the applied solution. For what seemed an eternity, I suffered through the torture. It was too late to stop the procedure. I was trapped, a now unwilling hostage until the bitter end.

The bitter end was indeed bitter. I looked like a blond Little Orphan Annie, only a bit taller. What a disaster! The kinky mass of tiny curls seemed set in concrete. How would I ever get a comb through it, much less make it look halfway presentable? I was too embarrassed to walk to the car, and facing school friends on Monday would be even worse. Talk about your bad hair day!

But the deed was done, and I was stuck with the hairdo to end all hairdos. The operator had done such a thorough job that it might be months before I would have my slightly naturally curly hair back again.

Just think, if permanents were really permanent, I would now look like a 70-year-old comic strip character!

- Florine Ledford Olive

It's a Helluva Place!

The weather-beaten house, two-thirds log, sat back from the road surrounded by shoulder-high grass, weeds and wild shrubs. Obviously empty, probably more than 100 years old, it had never had a coat of paint. Edgar Allan Poe could have written a great horror story about it.

That spring of 1920, when I was 6, my parents purchased this farm located eight miles north of Fort Wayne, Indiana, on the narrow, yellow clay Bethel Road that followed an ancient Indian trail from the village of Wallen about one mile away.

"What do you think of it Max?"one of them asked.

"It's a Helluva place," I answered in Dad's railroad language.

We moved later that summer. Dad had cut a path through the rubbish to the house and put a cover over the open well in back to keep us and the chickens from falling into our water supply. He also cleared a 50-foot path back to our bathroom, a shabby privy held together with a covering of vines.

That night, after we went to bed, we were attacked - by bedbugs. Millions of them were pouring out of the walls. We were their first fresh food in months. And they were smart, too. When Dad sat the legs of our beds in pans of kerosene to keep them from crawling on the floor to the beds, those pesky varmints crawled out the ceiling and dropped down on us. But we were there to stay. We persevered and finally sent them to bedbug heaven.

Livestock was purchased, cows, that is. Five head of them stood each night at the water tank I had filled, a water bucket at a time, and drank it down to the bottom. Then they turned to me to ask for more. I tried throwing stones at them to get them to stop, but Dad said that wouldn't do. It took water to make milk, and I was the power on the hand pump to supply the water. When the neighbors' cattle stopped in for a drink, that was too much. I wanted to shoot them with the rifle, but Dad said that wouldn't be neighborly.

Chickens ran everywhere. Rail fences didn't keep chickens confined, and woe betide the chicken that got in Mom's way during the day. We had chicken and dumplings for supper that night. This happened at least five times a week. The leftovers were eaten the other two nights. After 75 years, I'm still full of chicken, not my favorite food.

My sister Shirley, two years younger than I, couldn't seem to get her trips to the privy scheduled for daylight hours, especially in the wintertime. I dutifully lit the lantern and escorted her back to the privy time and again. Mom had suggested this was the thing for a big brother to do.

Wintertime in northern Indiana is rugged, with nighttime temperatures regularly down to zero and sometimes as low as 24 degrees below zero. Sleeping in the drafty second floor of a log house is an experience not to be forgotten. Before bedtime, you toasted your backside red behind the heating stove in the living room and then ran like mad up the stairs to plunge into an ice-cold bed covered with sheep's wool comforters. If it snowed during the night, you would wake up the next morning with a white blanket on your bed. It blew in around the windows. Now you brushed off the powdery stuff and dashed down the stairs to the living room stove, hoping the fire had lasted all night. The cold must have killed the germs. We stayed healthy. We survived.

After 10 years of this, the folks decided that my sister could not walk the mile and a half that I did to ride the interurban six

18

miles to and from Fort Wayne to get to high school - so we moved back to the city.

When the time came to go, I hated to leave the farm.

I must have been nuts!

- Max Kessler

Three Cheers for Out-of-Towners

When I was 12, I dreamed of becoming the most popular girl in school. People would run over each other just to sit with me at lunch, and everywhere I went, heads would turn.

I got my big break when I was picked as a cheerleader. Granted it was only for out-of-town basketball games, but who knew where it could lead? Maybe May Queen and then 8th grade class president.

This flurry of possible popularity lasted a week. Funny how much you can pack into a week when you're a budding teenager. Looking back, I realize the whole idea was doomed from the start. For instance, according to my diary notes, it's a fact that we knew nothing about cheering. And why were we to cheer only at out-of-town games? Possibly so only a few local people would see us.

After five of us were selected for the dubious honor, it was rumored that one girl was not allowed to associate with another member. So, casting aside my aspirations, I decided I would drop out. I wonder if Virginia remembers the great sacrifice I was making. I haven't seen her in 40 years, and I doubt it made much impact on her life.

The next day, things were evidently resolved. Mother was making a red skirt, and I was shopping for red pants---which caused a brief panic due to the absence of such a thing in our town of Ironton, Ohio. We were also informed that we must furnish our own ride to the games. There went my fantasy of riding along with the boys.

We practiced at one another's homes, in their bedrooms, because it rained every day. We had no coach and no list of cheers, and we only had a week to prepare for the first game. What were the teachers thinking?

I finally found my red pants, and at the end of the week we went to our first game. The entire experience must have been something I never wanted to think about again. I didn't write another word about cheerleading or basketball.

19

The only note I made was "I could just cry! The other team's cheerleaders turned out to be acrobats! Our team lost 12 to 24!"

I didn't get to be May Queen, and I was never a class president. But I did have a pretty pair of red pants.

- Jeannine Southers

Justice?

Life in New York City's South Bronx was neither luxurious nor serene. When my husband Bill was 14, he lived in a four-room apartment of a six-story walkup. He was the kind of kid who read Flying Aces and built model airplanes. More often than not, his small bedroom was a clutter of paints, glues, Japanese rice paper, small gas engines and airplane parts. His bed lay unmade for days, and balsa wood shavings curled everywhere.

One afternoon, there was a commotion at the threshold of the apartment door. He heard hollering and went to see an unknown woman chastising his younger sister. Though usually timid, Bill immediately became protective and shouted, "Leave my sister alone!" The woman began screaming, becoming incoherent, until Bill yelled, "Get out of my house!"

"Your house? This is my house and I'm your landlady!"

Bill clamped his mouth shut, as she hissed hoarsely, "Everybody is complaining to me about loud noises in the air shaft." She shook her fist at him.

He knew he was in trouble. This awful person would lose no time in harassing his poor working mother. For indeed, those sounds were coming from the testing of his engines, while he hung out his window to the air shaft.

An air shaft of the late 1930s was an opening between tenement buildings that allowed some light and air to filter into otherwise dreary apartments. Bill's noises were probably of the same decibels as today's ultra-loud boomboxes.

In desperation, he shrugged his shoulders saying, "If what they are bothering you about are my little engines---why they couldn't possibly make a really loud noise. I'll go get you one, and you can see for yourself."

He turned on his heel and went into his room, not realizing she had followed quickly behind him. With tiny engine in hand, he turned to see a face pale from shock. Her head was still, but her eyes rolled about, traveling the four corners of the room.

20

Then her whole body seemed to wince. As she attempted to recover, their irate landlady gave the impression that she had come upon something dangerous and was trying to extricate herself from it with as little movement as possible. Without looking at his engine, she left.

Two weeks later, the dispossess notice arrived. Bill's mother dispatched herself over to Uncle Dan, who was a court clerk and a minor politician. After she related the incident to him, Uncle Dan assured her he would take care of it.

When the court day came, both plaintiff and defendant presented themselves. Bill's mother simply told of how her fine son was interested in aviation and had this wonderful ability to use his hands with deftness to craft his models. The landlady countered with an invective about how Bill was destroying her building and its peace.

After consideration, the judge rendered his decision, ending with "Madame Landlady, if young men in this area would spend more time in constructive activities of this type rather than stand on street corners creating mischief, this city would be a whole lot better place. I find for the defendant. Case closed."

Such is the power of family values---and the value of powerful family friends.

- Hope Schene

The Canoe, the Canal and the Viper

Dr. Raymond, our scoutmaster, was a great advocate of overnight camping trips. He had some notion about boys developing self-reliance, resourcefulness, and most important, distancing themselves from sinful situations in general and pool halls in particular. Too, the Scouts owned a marvelous spot---the lodge at Lake Juliana.

Life was pretty relaxed on those outings. That was the innocent time before busybodies began structuring every juvenile waking moment, and aside from an occasional lifesaving class, we were very much on our own. Thus, on a hot and sparkling morning in 1933, four of us were sitting on the dock, dangling our feet in the water, doing exactly nothing. Bill Duncan, Beefy Crandall and I were long-time buddies, and on this morning were monitoring the troop's newest tenderfoot, Oscar Koegal.

We had been talking about a canal which had been rumored to exist on the other side of the lake, when Beefy said, "Let's go

21

look. Nobody's using the canoe, so now's our chance."

So we set out in a canoe that perhaps wasn't overloaded but did sit very low in the water. There were four boys, four paddles and one canoe, with not a shirt, shoe, canteen, knife or life preserver in the crowd. The assumption was that we could look after ourselves.

The lake was about two miles wide, and with three experienced paddlers, we made the crossing in jig time. Once on the eastern side of the lake, we cruised the shoreline, looking for the entrance to the small canal which had been dug between Juliana and a neighboring lake in the '20s, during the great land boom. Some visionary developer believed that many of the lakes in Polk County could be joined in some sort of Venetian linkage, and tourist-filled gondolas would be as thick as gnats. The project failed, but the canals remained.

After a few minutes, we found it, a passage about 30 feet wide through the underbrush, magnet to an unknown conquest.

"Want to try it?" I asked.

"Sure is choked with water lilies," Beefy said. "No use comin' this far without tryin,' though. Let's go."

"Okay. What about snakes?"

"SNAKES!! Don't say snakes to me!" Bill yelled.

"Okay, probably none in there anyway," Beefy said calmly.

Slowly, quietly, we paddled into the dense foliage. Clouds of insects swarmed every time we brushed against a bush. Beefy handled the bow, and I paddled and steered in the stern. After about 500 yards, the canal took a 45-degree turn to the right. The passage opened up just a bit, and before we realized where we were, we coasted into them.

Never before or since have I seen snakes like that. For about 50 yards, there was a water moccasin coiled on every lily pad, and several were cruising, looking for parking places. Even allowing for expanding memory of time long past, I know there were upwards of a hundred snakes within 70 feet of us. Some were flicking their tongues, testing this new and alien presence. The thick ugly brown ones lay very still, coiled as though posing for an encyclopaedia photograph.

We drifted. Quietly I asked Beefy, "Think we can turn the canoe around?"

"Not without bumping a few off their pads."

"Oh my God, WE'RE GONNA DIE!" Bill yelled.

"Shut up, Bill. You're disturbing the snakes," I said.

"You think I give a damn about disturbin' the snakes? What

about me?"

"Just hush. Beefy, you think we can each turn around in the canoe and head out?

"Doubt it. This thing's awful low in the water. I'd hate to capsize."

"OH MY GOD! " Bill screamed.

Throughout this, Oscar, looking like an undernourished Buddha cross-legged in the bottom of the canoe, said not a word. He was not, however, taking a nap.

Very slowly, Beefy and I began backing the canoe. We eased close to an occupied lily pad, and without warning, Bill raised his paddle and slammed it hard onto the back of a large moccasin.

"HOORAY!" he shouted and lifted the paddle straight above his head in a victory salute.

It was only when the snake slid down the handle and bounced off his hands that we realized that it had wrapped around the paddle at the moment of impact. It lay writhing in the canoe, obviously not too pleased, even though we had certainly given it the vessel's finest accommodations. Oscar had scuttled backward, was firmly in my lap and pushing hard. Bill dropped his paddle, screamed in panic and made a giant leap forward, almost knocking Beefy into the canal. Through a miracle, the canoe remained upright and afloat.

I asked Beefy to give his paddle to Bill and told Bill and Oscar that they were to keep that snake in the middle of the boat, period. Other than our unwelcome guest, there was not a snake in sight. It didn't require much imagination to believe that they were all heading straight for us. Herpetologists would have us believe the snakes were as frightened as four terrified boys. Hah!

Suddenly, Beefy pointed ahead and to the right. He yelled, "Tommy! Look!" On the bank was a trail that some fishermen had been using as a launching ramp. I began paddling, hard. As the bow touched shore, Beefy and Bill leaped out and pulled the canoe onto the sand. Oscar and I jumped into the waist-deep water and pushed, expecting every second to feel the hypodermic sting of lethal fangs.

We flipped the canoe onto its back, retreated and waited. Several minutes passed---nothing happened. Beefy looked at Bill and said, "Since you're the moron who caused this, I nominate you to flip the boat."

"Respectfully," said Bill. "I decline. Ain't no moccasin goin' to gnaw on my finger."

"You know," I said, "there's a good chance he isn't even poisonous. Most of them aren't. Bill could you tell if his head is triangular? Was the inside of his mouth white?"

Bill whooped. "Triangular?? Man, I ain't even old enough to take geometry and don't know nothin' about triangles. And I sure wasn't checking his dental work. You crazy, Tommy."

Beefy stepped to the canoe and with one swift motion flipped it over. There was no snake anywhere. Our battered reptile had slithered into the water and was gone.

Within two minutes, we launched and boarded the canoe and, through lily pads that hosted no snakes at all, made for the open water. Another five minutes and we were laughing and, by tacit agreement, decided that there was no point in burdening Dr. Raymond with the events of the morning.

- Tom Peacock

Mortification

Oh, what a horrible incident happened to me when I was 17 years old!

In early May of 1951, I went over to Chapel Hill for college entrance exams which included a physical before entering North Carolina's first four-year collegiate school of nursing.

Because the North Carolina Memorial Hospital had not been completed, 10 of us green RNs-to-be gathered in the University's School of Medicine Infirmary. We were secluded in a large, bare dormitory-like room with about 10 beds and one small bathroom.

The matronly assisting nurse asked us all to go into the restroom, strip to the nude and wrap ourselves into the large white sheet she handed us. We were to select a bed, place our clothes under the pillow and wait to be examined. We proceeded to do this with much blushing and giggling.

Then a very, very young (still wet behind the ears) intern, dressed in his glorious whites, entered the room. He commenced to give each of us a quick vital sign check-up with some probing and punching and feeling of our youthful bodies. All of us were embarrassed and very red of face.

As each female was processed, we were told to return to the ladies room and redress---physical completed.

To my utter surprise, I could not find my bra, size 30 AA, anywhere! I searched the room's every inch. Wrapping the sheet back around my 110-pound frame, I returned to that examining circus to look high and low, under the sheets, pillows, flannel blankets, everywhere. I finally dove beneath a white metal bed, seeking the contraption that Howard Hughes had invented for Jane Russell. (She desperately needed the engineered device for the movie *Outlaw* to keep everything contained; I didn't. I just wanted to locate my petite piece of lingerie.)

As I came up from under the bed, still braless, I saw Him coming down the aisle between the row of beds. The intern turned brain surgeon right in front of all the girls and the nurse. God Himself declared in a loud voice, "Is *this*..." From his stethoscope pocket, he whipped out my flimsy white badge of adulthood, "what you are looking for, Miss Smith?"

- Joy S. Burton

Beach Bums

High school girls will do things at the beach that they would never dream of doing at home. That became obvious whenever I had a houseparty at our cottage at Windy Hill near the wild and wonderful Myrtle Beach, South Carolina.

At home in North Carolina, we were very particular about the boys we dated. At the beach, it was a game to see who we could "pick up" for an evening's fun.

We roared hysterically when Barbara's dance partner at the pavilion waved at her the next day from a garbage truck. Neither her mother nor mine was amused.

All six of us were 14 when we snared 18-year-old and 19-year-old "hunks" for another brief escapade. Happily, we shared them, shagging the hours away. Unfortunately, the guys didn't catch on that they were a single night's entertainment. They found our cottage and came in for a visit the next day.

My mother was horrified at the younger one's tatoo and the "grown man's" greasy locks. She was tacit for the moment, retreating from sight.

Soon, Cathy and Barbara had lured them outside. Early that morning, those two had sneaked out of their window and set firecrackers off under the house, waking up the entire neighborhood. They had pretended to be as surprised as the rest of us. That explains why Cathy had asked Greasy Locks to help them get the screen back on their window.

Mother didn't see it that way. She caught him red-handed and red-faced holding the screen from their window. She promptly ordered him off the property.

To the shock of other parents, Mother insisted that, for our next houseparty, we bring our *own* boyfriends!

- Margaret G. Bigger

Where's Sesame?

I grew up in a kinder, gentler time, when proper etiquette was stressed. My high school, although public, was a "preppy" place.

At Hollins College, a women's college in Virginia, I had a problem because of my background. Most of the other girls there had gone to all-girl prep schools, so they couldn't understand why I'd stand and stand in front of a closed door. I was waiting for a boy to open it.

- Margaret G. Bigger

Potent Potions

As a freshman at Hollins College, I was intimidated by the confusing symbols and potions of Chemistry I.

Perhaps he thought he was putting us at ease, but our professor spent considerable class time telling us that accidents sometimes happen in the lab. If we were to splash a chemical on our bodies, we were not to try to wash it off with water. Instead we were to call out the name of the chemical, so that he or an assistant could quickly provide the appropriate antidote. I was *very* careful.

It must have been only the second lab period when a classmate began screaming. Hysterical, she was shaking her hand furiously. The professor rushed to her side. "What was it?" he hollered over her yelps.

She was too frightened to remember at first, then she bellowed, "Sodium chloride!"

- Margaret G. Bigger

A Learning Experience

One summer in the early '30s, I drove my mother, father and brother from Savannah to New York City to see the sights.

26

In the heart of the city, I suddenly found myself driving the wrong way on a one-way section of 42nd Street. Six lanes of traffic were coming at me fast. I backed up quickly and turned into a side street.

A policeman pulled alongside me. I told him we had just arrived in New York for the first time, and I was confused by the signs.

He must've been more confused than we were. On returning from the rear of the car, where he had looked at our license plate, he asked, "Where is G. A.?"

- Jim Shearouse

Baring More Than Your Soul

You would think that nothing would be more intimidating to a 19-year-old girl than a visit to a gynecologist's office. It's bad enough being wrapped in a sheet, legs placed in cold metal stirrups, as you wait nervously for the doctor to start an extremely embarrassing examination.

Dr. TeLinde, head of the GYN Department at Johns Hopkins, entered the room and stood at the end of the table where I was perched. It vibrated along with my shaking knees. "Now, young lady, I just want you to relax," he said in a kind, professional voice.

I looked at him and then past him to the open window behind. I could see the legs of people walking past. What if someone dropped something and stooped to pick it up? He would see me! I was mortified! "If you'd pull the shade down," I gasped, "maybe I could relax."

He laughed and patted my foot saying, "Who do you think is going to recognize you from this angle?"

- Harriet Orth

Learning to Drive

In 1939, my father bought a 1932 LaSalle, a 12-cylinder, dark green limousine. He purchased it to transport our family from the harsh city of New York to our gentler hometown of Baltimore. This gas-and-oil-consuming, eight-passenger monster was the pride of his life. On snowy days, when much newer cars were unable to move, he'd just turn the key and away he'd go, chuck-

27

ling all the way to our business, Stanley's Jewelry and Gifts.

At 16, I had obtained my learner's permit and was chomping at the bit to drive. He used to let me steer and shift gears while he drove, but actually getting behind the wheel and driving was another story.

Confidence wasn't my problem, because I had talked several of my dates into letting me drive their or their parents' cars. They wouldn't think of screaming at me, but they didn't own a LaSalle limousine that had been owned by a senator.

One early spring morning, he finally gave in and allowed me to sit in the driver's seat. He rode in mortal terror for three blocks and, as I approached the stop sign, he jumped out of the moving automobile, ran around the front of it, ripped open the door and pushed me over to the passenger seat. It must have been temporary insanity.

"I could have killed you!" I gasped. "Is this the way I'm going to learn to drive, with you running in front of a moving car? You scared me to death!"

Dad lit his Piedmont cigarette with shaking hands, as I sat there glowering at him. "This car is too big for you to learn to drive on," he said. "We'll get Uncle Louie's car. It's smaller, and you'll be able to see over the wheel better."

What he really meant was that, no matter how much he loved me, he wasn't going to let anyone mess with the LaSalle.

Uncle Louie came over in his wreck of a car---a faded green, rusting Chevrolet---accompanied by their oldest brother, Uncle Willie, a very nervous man. My dad and Uncle Willie were put in the back seat, and Uncle Louie drove to Reisterstown Road. He pulled over and told me I could now drive.

The car had bucket seats, but the driver's seat was just a shell filled with several throw pillows to fill up the hole. I sat down and disappeared to the floorboard. They fluffed up the pillows, but I had to sit on the rim edge, which was a bit difficult and most uncomfortable.

Uncle Willie almost went into cardiac arrest, when he realized they were going to let me drive. They hadn't told him what this excursion was for. He was babbling and very upset, begging them to let him out of the car.

I started the motor, put the car in first gear---and the ball on the shift came off in my hand! Hastily screwing the ball back, I shifted to second. With each shift of the gear, the ball would come off.

Uncle Louie had told Dad to sit quietly in the back seat and he would instruct me. He began, "Now Honey, put your foot on the brake and then the clutch when you start coming to a stop."

From the rear, my father yelled, "No! First you put your foot on the clutch, then the brake."

Uncle Willie screamed, "She's going to kill us! Let me out of here!"

"Be quiet back there!" demanded Uncle Louie. "You're making her nervous." An understatement for sure.

What with slipping off the rim, the ball coming off with each shift of the gear and grown men yelling at me, the car came to an abrupt stop. I had stepped on the brake, and my bottom fell into the seat, so I couldn't reach the clutch. Uncle Louie groaned as the gears stripped.

"Why can't you all stop screaming at me?" I cried. "I know what to do, but you are making me crazy!" Uncle Louie tells me one thing; Daddy another and Uncle Willie has been blubbering since I got behind the wheel. Now..." I said with determination, "I'm going to drive."

I adjusted the pillows, screwed the ball as tight as I could, put the car in first and drove down the street without stripping the gears but holding onto the wheel for dear life to keep from falling into the seat. All was quiet except for whimpering Willie. I managed to drive a couple of miles. But when I went to make a turn, they all went wild. I pulled over to the great relief of everyone.

Uncle Louie said I didn't need any more lessons on his car. I'd done just fine. Uncle Willie left town that afternoon, and Daddy came home with a migraine headache. My rear end took several days to feel better from the bruises made by the rim of the seat.

The LaSalle lasted until it became impossible to get parts. Even then, Daddy kept it parked behind the house, just to remember the good old times when it gave him such pleasure. I drove it only that one time.

There is a moral to this story: stick to driving cars owned by your boyfriends. They don't holler at you---only gasp.

- Harriet Orth

When a White Wedding Gown Meant Virgin

Dating was different in our day.

For many of us, chaperones were a reality. And we don't mean just at dances. We had to take them on dates---especially "single" dates, which automatically made it a "double" date.

The trick was to find the youngest chaperones possible: newlyweds, a big sister or a college senior if you were a freshman. The treat was to lose them.

Certain dating etiquette was generally understood.

Girls must wait for boys to ask them for dates. The only exception: Sadie Hawkins Day. For a Sadie Hawkins Dance, the girls could (but seldom did) choose the guy they had always wanted to go out with. They then must arrange transportation and pay for the evening's entertainment.

"That was the heck of it," said a former teenager. "For once, instead of throwing out hints, pining away or standing on your head to get a boy's attention, you had society's permission to call the man of your dreams and ask him to a dance. None of us ever did. Somehow that would be too obvious that we 'liked' him. Or maybe we feared the 'turn down' that boys had to face. I took a neighbor who had been a childhood friend, because everyone would know that I didn't have a crush on *him*."

Girls may not telephone boys. Never. Ever. Not even to ask a homework assignment.

One teenage girl of the '50s did admit using the telephone to get dates. "I would guess who might ask me for a particular Saturday night. In our 'crowd,' Wednesday was ask-out night. If he had not called by 8 p.m. that evening, I'd dial the boy's phone number, let it ring twice and hang up. That, I was sure, brought the fellow's attention to the phone and woke him up to the fact that he had not made the obligatory call. Within five minutes, he would be calling---*if* I'd guessed right."

Before the first date, a boy should meet the girl's parents. If he did not already know them, he was expected to shake hands with the parents and chat awhile before taking their daughter out of the house. Some guys shivered and stuttered during this intimidating encounter.

Even after a boyfriend had been properly introduced to her parents, one dating daughter in the early '30s was required to get to know him better before they could go out. This meant several parlor dates. After a while, Mama and Papa would discretely disappear. But when the hall clock chimed 10, he knew it was exit hour. If Mama and Papa got tired early, they'd turn the clock ahead a bit.

If the parents do not approve, the date doesn't happen. The girl's mother and father had to know the boy's family. If the dad did not like the boy's father, the girl could not go out. The same was true if he did not like the looks of the boy. Even if her parents were willing to take a chance on a newcomer, she could expect the question, "What does his father do?" And she'd better have a good answer.

"I remember screaming, 'I don't CARE what his father does. He's nice. I like him,'" said a woman recalling her youth. "My parents asked the same questions about my girlfriends, too. I thought it was silly. But once they proved to be right. A friend I hung around with frequently had a father who was a traveling salesman. He often took his wife with him and left his 15-year-old daughter and 17-year-old son at home alone. My friend's favorite 'sport' when I was over there was to dial a random number, and if a man answered, she'd talk 'sexy.' When my mother found out about the situation (not the phone calls), I was forbidden to go to her house ever again. I thought I had the meanest mother alive. But those kids must have done more than *talk* sexy; both of them *had to* get married when they were still teenagers."

No matter how often they date, the boy should come to the front door and speak with the girl's folks. Anyone rude enough to sit in a car outside and honk, expecting a girl to rush out and jump in would find himself without a date. A girl who was allowed out the door under such circumstances was not considered "well bred."

One seasoned citizen recalls his date's old man answering the door too suddenly. He had forgotten to throw down his cigarette before ringing the doorbell and stuffed it---and his hand---into a pants pocket. Burn. Stink. Smoke. Chills tickled his arm before the burning sensation hit his palm. His singeing pocket put out an aroma that only he could identify. If the older gentleman saw the smoke, he didn't mention it, but the youngster got out the door with his girl without ever showing his butt.

"Double date" before you can "single date." Different parents had different rules on how many double dates earned a single date. They had to be sure they could trust the boy with their daughter. Often, single dating was earned by reaching a certain age. Girls also had to earn the privilege of a "car date."

"My first car date was a disaster," said a woman in her late 50s. "My mother didn't know the boy or his parents, so the only reason she let me go was because she knew Harriet's mother.

Frank and I would be double-dating with Harriet and Joe, who was driving. The plan was to go to a baseball game. But as soon as I got into the Ford coupe, I realized we were not headed for Harriet's house. Joe was dating Eth. Furthermore, Eth didn't like baseball games. We'd go to a movie instead. But no one knew what was playing. Rather than buying a newspaper, we rode around to all five theaters in town to read the marquees. We chose one downtown. But Eth was being punished and had to be in by 10 p, m. My curfew was 11. So we left the movie early to get her home. Joe pulled up in front of a strange house. The next thing I knew, Frank had borrowed his mother's green Dodge and I was single-dating. A 'cheap date,' Frank knew where they were giving out free Cokes, so off we went.

"We arrived in front of my house about five minutes before curfew. We had a bet on what would be the number one Hit Parade song on the radio that night. As the first bars were played, he got out of the car to escort me in. My mother was livid and grew madder by the moment. She had called Harriet's mother and found out that Harriet was not with us. She had already jumped to the conclusion that we were 'parking' out front ('What will the *neighbors* think?') and could see that I was single-dating ('without permission!') in another car ('with a *stranger* driving'). But when she heard that we hadn't gone where we said we would be and had driven *around* (not straight to our destination and back), Frank was banished from my life FOREVER (in reality, for now)."

Never kiss until the third date---if then. This could be the act determining whether a girl was "fast," a derogatory term for being a "loose woman." If she allowed a boy to kiss her on the first date, the news circulated quickly among the males at school and usually seeped into the conversation of other girls. The guys would speculate as to whether this one might "go all the way." A girl's reputation was precious then, and easily tarnished--- sometimes unjustly by a braggadocio.

"Kissing was put at such a premium," said a woman from the time when a girl would never initiate a kiss, "that I kept a notebook on my dates, logging in the number of kisses, hugs and hand-holdings. And boys thought they were the only ones who knew how to 'score'!"

You-know-what is reserved for marriage. That's why brides wear white, girls were told, to signify virginity. Needless to say, the first night of a honeymoon was a very special event.

32

"In my day, it was romanticized so much," said a woman of the 50s, "that I thought I had to have a glorious gossamer peignoir set---white, of course---for that night and a different beautiful gown for every successive evening of my honeymoon. We would be gone two weeks. That's 14, which explains why I took five suitcases." She leaned over to confide something she'd never told before. "But the shock of my life was when those beautiful gowns stayed on about five minutes---if that."

If information were scarce (except via "whisper education"), advice was plentiful.
A popular booklet suggested that girls think of their bodies as the map of the Eastern United States. To allow a member of the opposite sex to touch New York was not nice, but Florida should be forbidden territory.
A grandmother told her granddaughters, "Never hold hands, it will lead to..."
A father warned his girls, "If sitting on the sofa, keep both feet on the floor, knees together."
But an understanding mother suggested that her daughters take advice from the top of a mayonnaise jar. It read, "Keep cool, but don't freeze."
The mama who always asked after a date, "How did you make out?" didn't know the new teen term for kissing (and more) was "make out."

Did you notice? Even our storytellers here confide only in *secret*!
- An anonymous compilation

33

ADULTHOOD'S LITTLE CRISES

Good Samaritan, That's Me!

A car had stopped behind me, blocking my exit from a bank parking space. At first I waited patiently, but as the car and I sat for a number of minutes, I tooted my horn. The other driver failed to move and I silently fumed.

Then I noticed the driver was slumped over the wheel, and I glanced wildly around, hoping to see someone, anyone, who might know what to do in a medical emergency. But there was no one in sight.

I stepped out of my car and walked hesitantly toward the stricken driver. Looking in the windows, I noticed two large-eyed toddlers in the back, while a female driver continued to lean over the steering wheel.

Feeling that time was of the essence, I jerked the car door open and grabbed the lady by the shoulder, as she screamed and raised up with pen and checkbook in hand.

- Jeannine Southers

That's the Army for You!

My prospective son-in-law, a recent VMI graduate, called our daughter one evening soon after the Army sent him to Fort Bragg. Joy wasn't home, so I opened our chat with "How are things going, Mike?"

"You wouldn't believe it," he said. "Ever since I was 5 years old, I've wanted to be in the Army. The greatest day of my life was the day I got commissioned. And what do you think they have me doing?"

"What, Mike?"

"This morning 235 guys came in for summer camp, and I've had to watch each one individually pee in a cup." He sighed with exasperation. "But at least they saluted me when they did it."

- Margaret G. Bigger

He Wasn't Wrestling With His Conscience!

At my college roommate's wedding reception in Tarboro, North Carolina, I was running my mouth when I heard a commotion behind me. I turned around to see Randy, my brand new husband, wrestling on the floor with the bride. People were screaming and hollering, and with all that chaos, it took me awhile to sort out what was happening.

It seems that, when the bride was feeding the groom that first bite of cake, all eyes were on the cake going into his mouth---except my husband's. He saw her short veil catch fire in the flame of the candle on the table. Randy jerked the veil. But it didn't come off (what with all the bobby pins), so he jerked again, jolting her to the floor. Then he jumped on top of her, banging the flames out with his hands.

He was a hero. I just didn't see it that way.

- Margaret G. Bigger

A Wedding Present

Dad and Mom were married June 23, 1913, at Warsaw, Indiana. Dad was only 20 years old. Indiana law required parental approval for marriage of a male under 21, so his father was there, too.

After the ceremony, they all took the local train the 15 miles west to his parents home in Bourbon.

Later that afternoon, Father Kessler said good-naturedly, "Well, Gilbert, now that you are a married man, I suppose you would like to show Hope (the new bride) how much of a man you are." He brought the much-used family boxing gloves from the house to the yard, where everyone was gathered and tossed Dad a pair.

Reluctantly, Dad put on his gloves. He knew what was going to happen. It had happened many times before. It happened again.

Proving the hand is quicker than the eye, Gilbert was flat on his back on the ground, looking up at his father's smiling face and his bride's shocked one. He said, "I slipped."

He didn't.

- Max Kessler

36

Heads Up!

Jimmy was full of himself and often got into mischief. He was among a lively group of fifth graders I taught at Warlick School in Ranlo, North Carolina, in the 1960s.

One afternoon, our class was playing softball. Jimmy threw a ball that grazed the top of my head and sent my fashion wig flying across the field.

At first there was dead silence. I believe the children thought my head had been blown off. But when they realized the situation, there was pandemonium. They fell on the ground with laughter, and children came running from other classes in all directions. Jimmy was petrified. But the look on his face set me to laughing, too, and I joined in on the fun.

For weeks afterwards, in the middle of a class, there would be a sudden burst of laughter. They were remembering the time I lost my head.

- Mary Hopkins

Picture Perfect

In a fatal automobile wreck, a man from Georgia, my home state, was badly mangled. The Atlanta undertaker could not tell what he looked like normally. He was dismayed, for there would be an open-casket viewing.

But on a visit to see the widow, he noticed a man's snapshot on the piano, and while she was out of the room, he slipped it into his pocket.

Well, when the widow came to look at the corpse, she gasped, "My God! My first husband's face on my second husband's body!"

- Jim Shearouse

Tell It to the Judge

At our "no fuss" wedding in Lodi, New Jersey, the judge was soberly speaking of the responsibilities of marriage in stentorian tones. My groom Bud was so rapt that when the time came to repeat his vows, he gave every one great emphasis, looking unwaveringly into the judge's eyes. In fact, he promised to love, honor and cherish *the judge*!

After being kidded for 27 years by his parents, who stood up with us, Bud has devised a quick response when queried about marital longevity. "It's simple," he says. "Just marry the judge and live in sin with your wife. Keeps the thrill alive."

- Sally DePriest

Icing on the Cake

I pouted a bit with my husband/employer for inviting a visiting dignitary home with us for supper.

"But it's my birthday!" I whispered, as I caved in to the idea. A startled look briefly crossed his face, but he suggested that I ride with our guest and said that he would be along in about 20 minutes.

After a pleasant evening and meal, my beloved ducked into the kitchen and re-emerged bearing a bakery cake box. "They were just closing," he explained sheepishly, "and this was the only one they had left."

Inside was an elaborately decorated cake that proclaimed to the world, "Happy Birthday Gertie"!

- Bet Ancrum

All He Wanted Was a Teal Shirt

One summer evening while my husband, Larry and I enjoyed the coolness of a mall in Myrtle Beach, he spotted a teal shirt hanging from a circular rack. "I think that's the color I've been looking for!" he said, examining one more closely. "Wonder what size I need?"

"There are some dressing rooms, " I said, pointing toward a back wall.

Unable to locate a salesclerk, he took two shirts to try on. The rooms, however, were locked. "Maybe I can reach across the top of the door and open it." He stretched from his tip toes. "Nope, can't quite do it."

We paced the aisles and scanned the store for assistance.

Presently, an image appeared in my peripheral vision: Larry's backside, with two shirts trailing behind. Like a puppy squirming under a fence with its prize, he was on all fours attempting to wiggle under a fitting room door!

He might've made it, too, if he hadn't been startled by "May I help you, Sir?" from a salesclerk towering at his feet.

- Betty Walker

The Woebegone Burglar

The shrill siren of my burglar alarm awakened me at 2 a.m. I jumped out of bed, grabbed and loaded my shotgun. With classic TV police drama technique, I searched my home, room by room. Reaching the hall, I found the front door open. The siren had evidently frightened the burglar away. Cutting off the alarm, I picked up my cordless phone and walked out to check my car.

Dialing 911, I asked for the police and said, "I've just had an attempted burglary. What should I do?"

The police operator began to ask questions.

Standing on the well-lighted front stoop in my underwear, shotgun in one hand, phone in the other---and with numerous neighbors peeking through their blinds---I saw the cat burglar.

It was Lovey, my door-opening cat.

- Paul Sagesse

The Great Baby Race of 1940

Whose baby would be first? Or did it really matter?

Those were important questions for two young couples who shared an old railroad apartment in New York City in the fall of 1940. During those nine months of happy anticipation, Jean and Glen McAlister became our close friends.

Jean and I shared the same due date, but she went to the hospital first. "False alarm," the doctor said and sent her home.

We rejoiced with Glen when their second trip resulted in the birth of Charles. We also gently teased him about the long hours he spent at the hospital. A ministerial student at Union Theological Seminary, Glen studied during the long waits between the brief afternoon and evening visiting hours. He was the friendliest, kindest and most humble man I had ever met. By the end of Jean's week-long stay, he had undoubtedly become well-known and admired by the hospital staff.

Two weeks later, my labor began. My husband was at his pre-war job in New Jersey, so Glen stopped studying for his Greek exam and called a cab. We seemed to crawl the 40 blocks up

Broadway to Columbia Presbyterian Hospital. I said, "I'm sorry we're causing you to miss your Greek exam. If the baby is a girl, she will be named Dorothy, Greek for 'gift of God.'"

"And she will be." He patted my hand, reassuring me.

When we arrived at the huge hospital complex, I was glad that he had been there twice before. He knew exactly where to take me. We stepped off the elevator at the umpteenth floor.

As we approached the desk, he was carrying my coat and small suitcase and had his arm protectively around me. The plump matronly nurse raised her head from her paperwork. Her welcoming smile became a look of disbelief and dismay. But she managed two words. "Mis-ter....Mc-Al-is-ter?"

- Lucy Almand Harrison

What's Romance Got to Do With It?

Bud actually never proposed. This romantic feat was accomplished via a long distance phone call from Kansas City to Charlotte. The conversation was between me and Bud's boss, Charlie.

During the actual proposal, Buddy was otherwise occupied in a men's room in a Kansas City Saloon. Charlie handed him the phone when he returned to the bar. And to Buddy's astonishment and probably horror, I joyously accepted the marriage offer. Before hanging up, we made plans to meet in Charlie's hometown, Tulsa, Oklahoma on the following Wednesday.

My darling mama refused to let me elope unaccompanied to the wild wooly Midwest and helped me select a suitable trousseau in record time. She also secured two plane reservations to Tulsa. Mama, knowing me too well, figured I'd just move in with Mr. A without benefit of clergy unless she were along to supervise the ceremony. How fortunate I was have her with me, since no groom was waiting to greet the bride-to-be at the terminal.

Thankfully, I remembered Charlie's last name and was able to phone him to come rescue us. He put us up in the Holiday Inn Buddy normally frequented and tried to reassure us that I hadn't really been jilted. Undoubtedly his star salesman had gotten tied up with a buyer, etc., etc., etc.

"Mr. Wonderful" showed up several hours later, explaining how he had lost his umbrella in Midland, had gotten a huge order in Odessa and had missed the turnpike exit to downtown Tulsa. Mom and I pretended to believe his every excuse and were genuinely relieved that he had even shown up.

On Thursday morning, we passed blood tests and obtained the marriage license. That evening, Charlie and his wife, Ginny, invited the three of us to their home for a pre-nuptial celebration. My "intended" tried to over-imbibe. "Bridegroom jitters," we tittered.

Charlie and Gin drove us to City Hall on Friday for the big event. Upon arrival, my betrothed refused to budge from the car, since he'd started having second, third and possibly fourth doubts about the whole idea.

My 90-pound mother finally prodded him loose, and we retired to extremely gloomy chambers where we were scheduled to exchange vows.

Through a rear door, out popped our justice of the peace. Hizzoner was even more diminutive than my teeny mama and was missing a limb. This prompted the groom-in-waiting to loudly whisper, "Is this one-armed paper hanger actually going to marry us?"

Although someone (perhaps his Mrs.) had quite nicely secured his empty sleeve with an enormous brass safety pin and attached a bright green Kleenex carnation to his lapel, I was beginning to have doubts of my own.

When he intoned "Dearly beloved," my beloved interrupted the proceedings with,"Leave out all the honoring and obeying and get to the point, man."

The judge, sensing an air of urgency, looked us both straight in the eyes and continued, "By the power vested in me by the great state of Oklahoma, I pronounce you husband and wife." That brief text was enough to legally unite us.

Our romantic interlude has entered its 33rd season. Each day together has been as exciting and---unnerving---as the day we were married.

- Susie Abrams

Saturday Morning Surprise.

Boxes of Girl Scout cookies lay abandoned on my rear stairwell. Haphazardly, they loomed in crevices and corners on each riser. Clearly a perverse crime had occurred mere inches from my back door.

I cautiously slipped my key into the lock and quietly entered our apartment. Utter silence, except for the clock's ticking, calmed my racing heart. However, the view outside the

41

bay window overlooking our deck and back stairs reinforced my terror---the cursed cookies were everywhere.

Holding my breath, I entered our bedroom to be greeted by deafening snores. Seemingly, my nude portly Prince hadn't budged since I'd left to go shopping.

"Honey, wake up!" I implored. "Some sex maniac is stalking Girl Scouts in our complex. Didn't you hear anything while I was out?"

Groggily, he replied, "Babe, some nut banged on our door and woke me. It must've been a joke, because when I opened up, no one was there."

"Buddy, were you wearing your glasses when you opened the door?"

"Hell, no. I couldn't even find my robe."

- Susie Abrams

English Hospitality

Before getting close enough to Stratford, it was clear that we had waited too long to find a bed-and-breakfast. I found myself getting a wee bit cranky, as I repeatedly reminded my husband to keep our rented VW Beetle to the left side of the road on turns. We were stopped by a light and looked over to see an old stone house that had a faded broken down sign hanging from a worn out chain. We could barely make out the word "Guests." Since Bill glories in the word "cheap," he quickly pulled up beside the curb at Fern Bank in Worcestershire.

The lady who answered the doorbell sweetly smiled. "There really are nicer places down the road," she said. But she quoted him a lovely low price, so Bill ignored her suggestion and hurriedly came out to get me to have a "look see."

After greeting me with friendly liking, she impulsively said, "Well, why don't you just come in and have a cupa with me."

As we gratefully trooped into the hall, I noticed two large parlor rooms on either side of a center staircase. There were some young men and women in both rooms having drinks. Our hostess directed us past the stairway to the back of the house, where we entered a bright kitchen. She put on the kettle and invited us to sit down, all the while keeping up a lively repartee.

Molly Bomfort was probably in her 50s, with gray-white hair and dancing blue eyes. She had a wonderful figure and wore a cashmere sweater and skirt that matched the exact purple color of her suede shoes. In the early '70s, that outfit was a bit dated, but Molly still seemed to have a flair for style and elegance.

After more good English tea, Bill climbed into his best funny element, getting her undivided attention. As we laughed more and more at his jokes, she began making highballs. We were old friends by the time we realized we were ravenously hungry."Oh, fine," said Molly, who suggested that all three of us drive to her favorite pub.

A pub in England is not just a bar. It's a homey place for the local inhabitants to catch up on the happenings of the day. As we entered, there was an uproar of greetings for Molly and much clamoring for her to "come on over." Bill and I went to an old wooden table by a window, while Molly and her all-male admirers went into a huddle. Every once in a while, one of her group would cut his eyes our way, shoulders shaking with laughter, and slap his thighs. We felt a bit uneasy, and they winked and poked at one another.

Soon Bill and I were really ready to retire and finally coaxed Molly back home. As we entered, there were other people in the parlors. Molly began again, "There really are much better accommodations just down the way, and besides, the beds aren't made."

Exhausted, we persuaded her that we would all go upstairs, make beds and not worry anymore about it.

The next morning, in her flowered silk robe, Molly cooked us the traditional English breakfast: bacon, eggs, fried bread and muffins with marmalade, juice and tea. After eating our fill, we parted with much "cheerio-ing."

As we were driving away, I looked back to see Molly holding her hand over her mouth, and I knew it just couldn't have been Bill's last joke that convulsed her with laughter.

After an uneasy silence, Bill said thoughtfully, "Did you hear a lot of doors opening and closing and people moving about last night?"

"Yes," I said, "and a lot of heavy breathing."

After an even longer silence, Bill burst out, "You know Honey, I think we stayed in a brothel."

"Oh wow," I sputtered. "Now I know why she tried to get rid of us. But what about that 'guest' sign?"

He chuckled. "So what would you have put up?"

- Hope Schene

The Fallen Woman of Hay Street

Mention Fayetteville, North Carolina, anywhere in the world, and chances are, someone will respond, "Are you familiar with Hay Street?"

Indeed! Hay Street abuts the historical Market House, where in 1789, the State Assembly adopted legislation chartering the nation's first state university, the University of North Carolina. To Olde Fayetteville (that's old with an e), it was the center of commerce, before department stores and specialty shops defected to the mall. Those were replaced by wig shops, pawn brokers, stores promoting the most garish type of clothing, food establishments reeking with the aroma of fried onions and places where a down-and-outer can exchange a pint of blood for the price of a bottle of Ripple.

Hay Street is home to old and established churches, the once elegant Prince Charles Hotel, the now decrepit train station that in better times was a hub of activity and movie theaters whose marquees have gone dark. But it's none of these past or present attributes that has carried the name of Hay Street to the far reaches of the world.

Rather, it's the two blocks of neon-lighted strip joints and bars that have made Hay Street infamous from the sands of the Sinai to the mountains of South Korea, from the jungles of Southeast Asia to the hamlets of West Germany and to every corner of this vast homeland. Hay Street, with its sleaze and prostitution, is a mecca of entertainment for the thousands of young soldiers who spend a tour of duty at nearby Fort Bragg and then ship out to far-flung bases around the world. Many of them are away from home for the first time and eager to taste the forbidden fruits of worldliness.

No wonder, then, that "Clean up Hay Street" became the battle cry of politicians seeking office in Fayetteville during the post-Vietnam years of the '70s and early '80s. But once the ex-candidates were in office, campaign slogans were replaced with the reality of dollar marks and question marks about how the job could actually be done.

As happens occasionally in this great land of ours, in November of 1981, the citizens of Fayetteville elected a mayor whose Methodist upbringing taught that promises made should be promises kept. The mayor attacked the problems of Hay Street with righteous zeal. Through his efforts, the city obtained an urban renewal grant from the federal government, enabling

44

construction of a transit mall in the first three blocks of Hay Street and the purchase of the entire fifth block, which later became the site of a medical complex.

The citizens of Olde Fayetteville were jubilant. A crowd gathered, creating a festive atmosphere, as the wrecking ball struck its first blow. In the same glad-hand spirit, a civic organization planned the groundbreaking for the transit mall as a media event. Because it was to occur on February 29 of that Leap Year, representatives of the local newspapers, radio stations and the city's one television channel were asked to participate in a leap frog race down Hay Street.

I was assigned to cover this gala event. And because I've always enjoyed writing about incidents that I've actually experienced, I recruited a colleague - at least 35 years my junior - as my leap frog partner.

Sam and I took our mission seriously, slipping away during rare newsroom lulls to practice how we would bring glory and the leap frog trophy to *The Fayetteville Times.*

The day for the race dawned bright but cool. The sheer bulk of necessary clothing hampered our carefully practiced form. Still, we were running a close second, when I felt a sharp pain in my right knee. It happened mid-air, as I narrowly cleared the slouched form of my partner. When I touched the pavement, I rolled over, unable to bear the weight on my leg.

We lost the race, and I got a free ride to the hospital emergency room. Until that day, I'd never seen a doctor speechless. But this one stared, mouth agape, as I explained how his 60-year-old patient had broken her leg in a leap frog race.

That was the easy part. The real challenge came when folks at Workmen's Compensation wanted an explanation for my claim. Yes, I was on assignment when the accident occurred, although I ended up the subject of the story instead of the reporter---much to the chagrin of City Fathers, who for once had hoped to get a positive story on the much maligned Hay Street.

Eventually, the insurance reps were satisfied, the bone repaired itself and the transit mall proceeded on schedule. But this is how I will forever be known in Fayetteville as "the fallen woman of Hay Street."

- Ellen Scarborough

BRINGING UP JUNIOR & JILL

New Mom's Christening
or
I Didn't Know the Gun Was Loaded

I gingerly changed my newborn's first diaper and...
SQUIRT! Right in my face.

Well, I smirked to myself, *next month the baptism will be on you.*

- Lucille Thompson

At a Loss for Words

When my son, Jay was almost 5, he came to me with the most serious questioning expression. "I know that the baby comes from the mother's body," he said, "but everybody keeps telling me that I look like my *daddy!*"

- Beth Tate Smith

Pooh Bear

When our youngest daughter Martha, celebrated her second Christmas, my brother Vernon sent her a Winnie-the-Pooh bear. He was a wonderful Pooh bear, putty colored, soft and cuddly, dressed in a bright teal sweater. Martha finally got the big decorated box undone, and I exclaimed excitedly, "Oh, it's Pooh!"

She immediately ran to the powder room, threw him into the toilet and flushed. Of course, the bathroom was soon flooded with a stuffed bear in the commode.

Martha was being potty-trained and thought Pooh was something else.

- Joy S. Burton

Getting It Right

As an anxious first-time mother, I worried that the three tiny holes in the rubber nipple of the bottle were too small to let much formula through. Carefully, I heated a needle and enlarged the holes, only to have the milk pour out in choking streams. I ruined several nipples before surrendering to the urge to consult authority.

"Dr. Walker," I asked, "just how important is it to get those holes the right size?"

"*Extremely* important, Mrs. Ancrum---with the first baby."

- Bet Ancrum

We're Not Really All Brothers

My sons, ages 2 and 5, went down the sidewalk together to see their newborn neighbor. When they returned, 5-year-old Andrew reported in wonderment, "Mama, Mrs. Toney's baby is so new it's still a girl."

- Bet Ancrum

As Others See Us

After the noon-time kindergarten carpool run, I decided to treat my 5-year-old son, Shepherd, to a hot dog and milk shake at Roses' lunch counter.

Shep, unaware that few people ask grace aloud in public, went into his customary "God is great, God is good..." routine, and even the waitress paused reverently in her tracks.

I basked sanctimoniously in the murmur of approval from nearby diners, until Shep followed his closing "amen" by clinking his milk shake glass against mine and pronouncing distinctly, "Well, cheers, Mom!"

- Bet Ancrum

Anatomically Incorrect

My husband and I used accepted anatomical names in vocabulary-training our children (urinate, not pee pee).

When I brought our second child, Johnny, home from the hospital, his 3-year-old sister, Ginny, commented on every detail of his appearance: First, "He's red like my blanket." And later as I was changing him, "He has a Johnny-talia, not a Ginny-talia."

- Anonymous

Pause for Refreshment

The soda shop at the Post Exchange of the Air Force Base in Madison, Wisconsin, was crowded and noisy with enlisted men, when my 2-year-old son and I came in for refreshments. The boisterous camaraderie became somewhat subdued as a colonel entered, took a seat beside us and ordered.

From the side of my eye, I saw the enlisted men muffling their mouths when my little fellow said to the colonel, "Don't spill your milk shake, honey."

- Frances Eppley

Macho Michael?

Michael, age 4, was late for Sunday dinner, and my parents had come for the day to Charlotte from Camden, South Carolina.

Finally, he arrived, huffing and panting. "Sorry," he said, "but Eddie pushed me down."

His father and grandfather reacted with macho pride. "Well, I hope you hit him back," said his dad.

"You stood up for yourself, didn't you?" asked my father.

You never saw two men back down so fast when Michael said, "No. You see, him was only two."

- Katherine Kennedy McIntyre

The Plunge

We had just arrived at our motel at the beach, and I was getting luggage out of the trunk, when my three-year-old son George disappeared.

I dropped my watch off my arm and raced for the swimming pool. There he was, face down on the surface. I dived

49

in to raise him up and put him on the side. He must've been holding his breath, for he wasn't even strangled.

Other motel guests gathered around him, as he began to cry. "Are you all right?" one said.

George pointed at me. "He pushed me in!"

- Bob Welsh

Baby's First Word

Our precious only child, Joy, stood at a footstool in our den, looking at her favorite picture book. She touched her little finger to the cat on the cover and said, "Kit-ty."

"Did you hear that? Did you hear that?" my husband exclaimed, jumping up from his chair. "She said 'Daddy'!"

- Margaret G. Bigger

You Need WHAT?

When my four children were growing up, I relished my moments of relaxation. One day after hanging out the laundry, I took a few minutes to lounge in the sun but was interrupted by my 10-year-old son Devin asking for chocolate milk. I told him he could make it; the recipe was on the box.

First he called out the kitchen door to ask where the measuring cup was, then he couldn't find the cocoa.

Just when I thought he must have all the necessary items assembled, he yelled, "Do we have any yield? I need two cups."

- Jeannine Southers

The Boy's Room

"...and his tools are all over the bedroom," I complained to my mother-in-law, hoping for some sympathy---or perhaps some advice on managing my new young husband.

She smiled with understanding over my predicament and said, "Do you know what is worse than a dirty boy's room? It is a clean boy's room, because it means the boy isn't living there."

- Katherine McAdams

Relatively Speaking

My parents in Eastern North Carolina always opened their big farm house to visiting out-of-town fellow Primitive Baptist members. After my wife and I moved to the Piedmont, we were expected to do the same, which crowded our family of four.

When my oldest daughter, Patricia, about 10, was playing in the yard with a girl from one of those visiting families, the other child kept referring to my father as "Brother Richard." Primitive Baptists always address each other as "brother" or "sister" as a bond of Christian love and fellowship. Patricia, who attended a Missionary Baptist Sunday school, didn't know this.

So she finally put her hands on her hips and said almost contemptuously, "How can he be your brother when he's my granddaddy?"

- Selby A. Daniels

Out of the Mouths...

Once a month in the 1930s, our truck body manufacturing plant in Fort Wayne, Indiana, had a party for everyone, with a buffet and beer. Those parties were on Friday night and lasted as long as anyone wanted to party and the beer held out.

I had too much beer one night and, fortunately, wife Millie had the car and picked me up. Saturday morning, I finally got out of bed, had some black coffee and slowly made my way toward the garage to get the car to grocery shop. Millie and 4-year-old son, Roland, were waiting for me by the driveway.

With the whole neighborhood working in their yards, Roland, pointed to a "glop" beside the driveway and asked in a loud voice, "Mommy, is this where Daddy was sick last night?"

- Max Kessler

The Runaway

A dispute with our 4-year-old son, Roland, had not been resolved to his satisfaction, and he announced he would run away. We told him we thought this might be a good idea, if he didn't like living with us anymore.

He decided he would go, so we helped him pack a paper bag

of the clothes he wanted along and made a sandwich for him to carry in another bag, so he wouldn't get hungry. We bid him goodbye at the front door, and he was off, with a sack in each hand, down Fort Wayne's Bowser Avenue that warm Indiana spring day.

About 15 minutes later, a neighbor who lived a short distance down the street called us. "Is there a problem at your house?" he asked.

"Well, we don't think so," I replied, "but we did help our son pack his things when he decided to run away."

"I thought you might say something like that," he said. "Roland just rang our doorbell, and when we answered he asked, 'Would you like to have a nice little boy live with you?'"

- Max Kessler

Mom's Lesson in Telling Time

When my son Cam was in high school in Salisbury, North Carolina, I learned a lesson in negotiating.

One weekend after Cam had attended a homecoming dance on Friday night, we were discussing the time for him to be home the following night.

I was trying to exhibit proper authority when I said, "Since you were out late last night, you should be in by 11:30 tonight."

After a few minutes of verbal positioning with Cam pressing for 12:30, he finally suggested, "Mom how about we split the difference, making it 12 midnight."

Not wanting to be too hard on my son, I agreed, smug that he had not completely won.

Then he called out over his shoulder, "Oh and Mom, I'll probably be 15 minutes late."

- Beth Tate Smith

If You Knew Bonnie Like I Knew Bonnie...

From her very first month, our daughter Bonnie was determined to have her own way. Every day was a challenge. She hated to be dressed, and just getting a diaper on her was a fight to the finish. Usually, there was a little bit of my blood on the diaper from the safety pins. She only kept her clothes on for a few minutes after she was put in her playpen. Everything went over the side, including her ribbons. A born nudist.

Just before Ricky was born, we moved into a two-story house in Baltimore. Bonnie was not yet 2. Within 15 minutes, she got her head caught between the iron railings which protected the concrete steps leading to the basement, tumbled down the stairway indoors, and then fell outside and skinned both knees. Believe me, having the hell scared out of you can bring on a baby! I called my mother to come get her.

One morning, I came downstairs to get a bottle for Ricky and was greeted by the worst mess imaginable. My little bandit had taken all the eggs, a bottle of French dressing and a few boxes of chocolate pudding and tried to mix them all together. The slimy combination was still dripping off the kitchen table onto the chairs and the floor I'd washed just a few hours before. Chocolate fingerprints were everywhere. It was nauseating. Bonnie had climbed back into her crib, so her room was a mess, too. Her explanation: "I baked you a cake." Immediately, I called Mother to come get her.

Not too long after that, I heard Ricky crying. They were in for their afternoon naps. When I walked into her room, I almost fainted. Bonnie had decided to do Ricky's nails with blood red fingernail polish. She had painted him up to his fat little elbows and poured the rest over the top of his strawberry blond head. Of course, I thought he was bleeding, and it scared me to death. "Mother Dear," I wailed on the phone. "Come get Bonnie."

And how did my poor darling mother cope with my rambunctious, mischievous child?

Quite well. Bonnie was an angel at her house.

- Harriet Orth

Don't Fence Her In

Sometimes, when Bonnie and Ricky were both taking naps, I'd lie down from sheer exhaustion. Bonnie would check to see if I were asleep and somehow lift the screen door latch and take off. The only way I could find her was to follow the clothes she removed on her flight to toddler freedom. Finally, after feigning sleep, I followed her. I wanted to know how she was unlocking the hook that I had to stand on my tiptoes to reach. She was getting the broom out of the closet at the top of the cellar steps, lifting the latch and returning the broom. This child was only 2! We replaced the hook with one that had to be pulled back to open. She got out anyway. She would push our heavy lounge chair to the door and stand on the top of the back until she could open the latch. Of course, she pushed the chair back before taking off.

We finally decided, to preserve my sanity, that we should put up a high fence in the backyard. As the men were installing it, Bonnie was climbing over it.

- Harriet Orth

Good For What Ails You

Nine months after we moved to Augusta, Georgia, our second son Marc was born. He teethed very early, and his doctor prescribed a half a baby aspirin for the pain.

We were at work when the maid called rather frantically. "I put Bonnie and Ricky in for their naps, and when I went upstairs, I found an empty bottle of baby aspirin. What should I do?"

My husband ran out the door for the car and raced home to get the kids. I met them in the emergency room, beside myself with worry.

The doctor didn't pump their stomachs, because we didn't know how much time had elapsed since they had consumed the bottle of aspirin, which had been full except for the one pill Marc had taken. "Make them drink water to dilute the medication. Get as much into them as you can," he said with a solemn look. "Check their breathing through the night, and if there's a problem, bring them in."

Both little bellies were so distended from all that water, I was afraid they would explode. I sat up all night, making sure they were breathing, terrified that they might die.

The next morning, both seemed to be fine. Bonnie awoke first. "That Ricky is so selfish!" she said. "He only gave me one."

- Harriet Orth

The Love Nest

Leonard, my brother, had a very nice efficiency apartment during his bachelor days in Baltimore during the early '60s. One of his friends, married to a beautiful woman and the father of three children, asked to borrow the apartment for the weekend. It didn't sit well with Leonard, who was not in favor of married men running around. His friend begged him, so he relented and handed over the keys.

Leonard's whole attitude changed toward this man. He started to avoid him. When the guy called for a handball game or tennis, my brother would make up an excuse not to go.

All of them were at the same wedding, when Leonard saw his friend's wife making a beeline for him. The guilt of lending his apartment to her husband had him looking for the nearest exit.

She was too fast for him, though, and threw herself in his arms, giving him a resounding kiss. "You were such a doll loaning us your apartment!" she gushed. "Getting away from the kids was the best vacation we ever had!"

- Harriet Orth

Questions, Questions, Questions

Have you ever noticed how little children, who barely know how to talk, can make you feel like you should have waited at least another 20 years before having them?

You start out with the misconception that since you were a child once, came from decent, loving parents and have a deep desire for motherhood, you'd do a good job and have all the answers. Ha!

Once toddlers can form a sentence, your education begins. It doesn't matter if you have a doctorate in child psychology when their questions are fired at you:

"Who turns the moonlight on?"
"Why do you sit down to pee pee?"
"Can you hear the baby inside your tummy talk?"
"How did he get stuck in there?"
"Why can't I see God?"
"How come I'm me?"
"Why is ice cold?"
"Is Grandma going to cut new teeth?"
"Why does it take so long to grow up?"
"How come I have to eat something I don't like?"
"What's inside my skin?"
"What makes my arms move?"
"What does the tooth fairy look like?"
"How come there are so many Santa Clauses?"
"Why do I have to sleep alone, when you can sleep with

Daddy?"

Now here's my question: If Dr. Spock was so smart, why didn't he give us the answers in his book?

- Harriet Orth

No Joy Rides on the Choo-Choo

Our train to Baltimore was supposed to stop in Greenwood, South Carolina, for only five minutes at 10 p.m. Five minutes? Right. Ten o'clock? Wrong by two hours!

Because it didn't stop in Augusta where Seymour and I lived, we had made the two-hour drive, so I could take the children to Baltimore to visit our families. Money was tight for us in the mid-'50s, so this would be our first trip in two years.

Trying to keep three active but tired and cranky kids occupied wasn't easy. They were 2, 5 and 7. Seymour didn't buy a ticket for 5-year-old Ricky, even though the rules said a half-fare was required at 5. Under that, they could ride free, although we had to pay extra for seat reservations. This made me very nervous, because Ricky knew he was supposed to have a ticket, and I hated the idea of having to lie.

When the train finally got in after midnight, my four beautiful leather suitcases were thrown onto the train, and we were whisked aboard with barely time to say goodbye. Seymour handed each of the kids a pack of gum and admonished them to be good. Then off we went.

The car we entered was already dark with almost everyone asleep. The conductor showed me and little Marc to one double seat and took Bonnie and Ricky to the other end of the car. So much for seat reservations! Within a few minutes, they were both back with me, very unhappy with the situation. I sent them to their seats, begging them to be quiet and respect the fact that people were sleeping. I could hear them fighting over who was going to sit next to the window. A general grumbling erupted throughout the coach. When the conductor came by, I asked him about the reservations we had paid for.

"Well, mam, with all these people asleep, it would be difficult to ask them to move so late at night," he said.

"If you expect them to stay asleep, you'd better find me some seats together, because my kids will be running back and forth all night." As I spoke, Bonnie came screaming down the aisle because Ricky had hit her. More grumbling from the passengers. Some were looking daggers at me for my unruly children. He took in the situation. "I'll see what I can find for you."

All four of us squinched in one seat, with the children pushing and squirming for space, was not very comfortable, so I was glad when he returned with a happy smile.

"We have a private car with Atlanta high school graduates on their way to Washington. They said you could sit in their car. None of them are asleep, but at least you will be together."

As he lifted Marc out of my arms, my skirt went up with him, and I grabbed Marc back. My child went back and forth between us in a tug of war, with my skirt going up each time. Marc had dropped his gum in my lap, so we were glued together. Until the gum finally started to stretch out like an umbilical cord, · I didn't know what the problem was. The conductor must have thought I didn't trust him to carry Marc and couldn't believe I was being so difficult.

The car with the graduates was noisy with guitars playing, kids singing, laughter and horseplay. My children were delighted and became new toys for the group to play with. One of our four suitcases had been filled with books, blankets, crayons and snacks for the 16-hour trip. The teens took turns reading to my brood and never slept. One of them returned Marc, who had finally fallen asleep. I spent the rest of the night trying to get the chewing gum off the seat of his pants and my skirt.

The snacks had been consumed almost immediately. By the time we got to Washington, where we had an hour layover, we were all starved. I had planned to get breakfast on the train while we rode to Baltimore.

Just then, the conductor came back to say they were detaching the car we were on. We would have to go forward, and he'd find us as seat. A seat was right! Now I had all three on top of me in half a seat plus the suitcase under my legs. The dining room was impossible to get into, because all the people who boarded in D.C. had the same idea.

The conductor reappeared and took us back to the car we had to vacate. It remained because of the number of passengers who had gotten on in Washington. Each move involved the other three suitcases being transported to whichever coach we were on. I imagine that conductor was relieved to be done with us when we finally arrived at the Baltimore station.

My brother was supposed to meet me at the train, but when we got off, he wasn't there. Three kids, four suitcases, and no Leonard! I couldn't believe there was nobody to meet us after the rotten trip I'd had. I was completely exhausted, and we were all starving hungry. There was not even a red cap in sight to get my baggage upstairs to the main waiting room, so I could phone to let them know we had arrived.

I warned the children not to budge, while I went up the steps to find some help and prayed my three Indians wouldn't get on a departing train. For once, they listened to me, and a red cap got us to the main floor. I gave him $2. He didn't seem too happy about that.

"Here, Bonnie," I said, handing her some change. "You're my big girl. You can call Grandma and tell her we're here." I wrote the number on a piece of paper and directed her to the phones. She didn't really want to do it but reluctantly obeyed.

She had only been gone a minute, when Ricky decided he had to go to the bathroom immediately. That was not surprising after the amount of ice water he had consumed on the train. I couldn't abandon the spot Bonnie would return to, and I certainly wasn't going to leave Marc by himself. I pointed to the men's room, and he went off in that direction. I was getting a little frantic with my children all over the place.

Ricky came running back. "It costs a dime to get into the bathroom," he whined.

I searched my purse, but I had given Bonnie my change, and I didn't have one for my poor Ricky. By then, he was holding his crotch and jumping around with tears in his eyes. "Crawl under the door," I said.

He raced back to the men's room like a bat out of hell.

Bonnie returned to say that my mother's phone was busy.

"Where's the change?" I asked.

She had bought candy and eaten it quickly so she wouldn't have to share. What a little minx!

The only thing to do was get a cab and go. I was so tired and hungry and burdened down with suitcases and children that all I wanted was to be done with this miserable situation.

Another red cap carried my luggage outside. I took out $2. "That's $4," he said.

I complied, but since I had very little money, having been taken like that really hurt. I wondered if I had enough left to pay the cab driver.

An amiable, smiling cabby put our baggage in his trunk. We all sat back, and I heaved a sigh of relief.

"Have you ever heard of the singing cab driver?" he quipped.

"If you sing one note, you will have a hysterical woman back here," I said and then told him of my horrendous trip.

58

"I'm afraid to tell you what it's going to cost to get you to your mother's," he sadly said. "But since the red caps took you so badly, I won't charge you for the suitcases."

When we got to my parents' house, my mother was sitting on the porch with a worried look. "Where's Leonard? He's been waiting for you all morning."

"That's what I'd like to know!" I said. "I can't believe he wasn't at the train to meet me."

"Train? He's at the bus depot!"

That was the end of the trip going up, but going back was even worse.

Bonnie decided she wanted to stay with my parents and not return to Augusta with us. I gave her the whole week to make sure this was really what she wanted to do, but she was adamant about staying.

During the week, I checked and found there was a train that would get us into Augusta at 9 a.m. instead of the one that would have arrived in Greenwood at 3 a.m. But they wouldn't refund my fares until I returned to Augusta. This meant I had to buy new tickets, using up all but a few dollars, which I needed for drinks on the train.

We were kissing goodbye when Bonnie chickened out. "I want to go home with you, Mommy!" All she had on was a sundress, panties and sandals. Her other clothes were at Mother's and Daddy's house. Of course, I didn't have a ticket for her. My parents had only a few dollars, but they gave me her fare. I could buy a ticket from Baltimore to Washington en route, but then I had to purchase another for the Augusta leg in Washington. For that, I would have to stand in line at the dispatcher's window during the one-hour layover.

Seating the children in the waiting area of the Washington station, I tried to buy Bonnie's ticket. The dispatcher acted like I was absconding with my own child. I could hear my threesome fighting with each other from across the vast room, and that idiot was delaying me so that we almost missed the train. This time, I couldn't afford to buy Ricky a ticket.

We made it with only seconds to spare. Once again, I wasn't able to get the four double seats I needed for the children to stretch out for the long trip. We opened the suitcase packed with six sandwiches, the boys' sweaters, blankets and games and a sweater for me. The train was very cold, so I had to give Bonnie my sweater. In no time, they ate all the food. I was hungry, freezing and poor.

The man in the seat across from us was stationed at Camp

Gordon. The only reason I can remember his name is that it, too, was Gordon, Sgt. Gordon. His head was as bald as a light bulb, and this seemed to fascinate Ricky. Finally Ricky whispered to me, "Mama, how come that man hasn't got any hair on his head?"

No easy question, that one. "I tell you, Ricky, he has a very bad little boy, and if you don't settle down, I'm going to look just like that!"

Ricky kept going back and forth for the ice water that was right behind the sergeant's seat. We were talking when suddenly Sgt. Gordon sat straight up, shocked by the cold little wet hand that ran over his scalp as Ricky passed by. I was mortified!

Ricky took the seat behind me. I followed and slapped his hand. "How could you do such a thing?"

"You hit me! I'll get even with you!" he said, crying. "Wait 'til I tell the conductor that I'm 5 years old."

"You tell the conductor that, and he will stop the train and put you off, because I haven't any more money, and I can't buy you a ticket." I couldn't believe he would pull this on me, but who knows what children will do?

Later, the conductor came by, and I held my breath, praying Ricky would not carry out his threat. When he called, "Conductor!" my heart jumped down to my shoes. I felt like I was going to faint. "How come you lock the men's room every time we stop?" he asked innocently.

The conductor gave me a sweet smile and explained it to him. I knew that he knew Ricky was 5, but he never mentioned it.

When the man was gone, I said, "Ricky, if you know what's good for you, you will go to sleep. I don't want to hear another word out of you. Do I make myself clear?"

He settled down and finally fell asleep. They were all sleeping when we stopped in Charlotte. There was no place on the train to buy even a cup of coffee, and my stomach was growling. I gave all the money I had left to Sgt. Gordon, who got off to run up to a diner.

Almost as soon as he was out of sight, the train began pulling out of the station! The sergeant was being left behind! Here this nice man was doing me a favor, and I was afraid he wouldn't get to his destination. What I didn't know was that we had an hour layover in Charlotte to switch tracks three times. Whenever we lurched forward, my guilt feelings magnified. By the time he got back, I was a nut. But I was a happy nut, for he brought back sandwiches, coffee and some fruit.

Finally we made it to Augusta. Once inside the depot, I told the children to stay in one place together. "Don't speak to anyone, not one soul, while I call your father," I said in my most authoritative voice.

I phoned Seymour to ask him to pick us up, but his assistant said he had gone to the post office, which was in the train station. We had left Baltimore at 5 p.m. and it was now 10 a.m. All I wanted to do was collapse, and now I had to wait 'til he got back before he could come get us.

I explained to the children why we would have to wait. Ricky, who had not said a word after that incident on the train slyly said, "I saw Daddy at the post office. But you said not to speak, so I didn't tell you."

- Harriet Orth

CRISS-CROSSING PATHS WITH . . .

Changing Jobs

The talkative young lady who came to sweep my hospital room explained that she was taking another job. Elaborating further, she said, "He's a dentist---pulls teeth. He's a big extortionist."

How true! How true!

- Clare Barry

Pretty Trashy, If You Ask Me

In the '50s, my friend, Mac was showing off one of the features in his new house, a trash compactor. He threw in a bunch of garbage and proudly removed a perfect cube.

When I asked what he intended to do with it, he said, "I'll wrap it up with a red ribbon," he said, "and throw it in my pickup, drive uptown and park. Somebody will steal it in five minutes."

- Faison Barnes

Lawyers Vs. Attorneys

In our Methodist Men's Class, we have an extensive mixture of professions and interests. As an introduction, our teacher, Everette, usually has comments about who's attending that day.

One Sunday morning, he said he'd noticed that the three lawyers in our class were all present. "Two lawyers and an attorney, that is," he added. "I was told that the difference between an attorney and a lawyer was $130,000."

"$135,000," the attorney corrected him.

- Jim Shearouse

Music?

During his sermon at our United Methodist Church a few Sundays ago, Bishop L. Bevel Jones told this story about himself.

Back in his early preaching days, he occasionally sang a song during his sermons. One Sunday, he did a few verses of "My Old Kentucky Home." He noticed that a lady in one of the front pews suddenly started crying.

Shaking hands with her as she left the church after the service, he said, "I noticed you were crying when I was singing. Are you a Kentuckian?"

"No," she answered. "I am a musician."

- Jim Shearouse

Not Even a "Merci Beaucoup"

My friend, Virginia, had been struggling hard to translate a letter for a library patron. It was in French. Finally she called the lady who had made the request.

"I have the translation," she told her. "The letter reads, 'Yes darling, it is possible for a man to love two women at the same time.'"

Click. The patron hung up.

- Katherine Kennedy McIntyre

Well, It's All Education

Fellow librarian Dot took great pride in a new section she had worked on for teenagers. She called it Facts of Life, a special collection with emphasis on achieving a wholesome sex life.

She was ready for the teenagers. I saw her talking with a young man about 14 and watched her lead him to the section. She pulled down *Attaining Manhood* and *Facts of Life and Love for Teenagers*. He seemed to like the books and perused them enthusiastically.

Dot asked, "Are these ok?"

"Yes, ma'am," he answered. "I like them a lot. But I don't see nothin' in them about factory life."

- Katherine Kennedy McIntyre

Introducing...

Will DePass was a popular man in our town. He was proud of being asked to make a major introduction at our Camden High School assembly in Camden, South Carolina.

The celebrity he was to introduce was General Charles Summerall, the new President of The Citadel.

We students were awed by the sight of the uniformed general on the stage.

Will DePass rose nervously. "I would like you to meet one of only six full generals in our country's history, General George Washington."

- Katherine Kennedy McIntyre

Drivin' Mr. Denny

My husband, Hundley, owns a limousine service. He invited his black friend, Denny, over to see the new office building that houses the cars. Denny arrived driving a mud-spattered Cadillac. Used to cleaning limos, Hundley ordered, "Drive in here, Denny, and I'll wash your car."

"What? Oh, okay," agreed Denny, sinking into a comfy chair. He watched my husband soap up his "wheels."

Denny smiled, kicked off his shoes and called out, "If he could see you now, man, ol' Jeffe'son Davis would turn in his grave."

- Lucille Thompson

Thanks, Nurse!

A nurse friend of mine commented that she was often amazed at how creative people were at naming their newborns. She remembered one mother who just could not decide what to call her baby, and, as usual, the hospital put a bracelet on the child with the identification "Female Jones."

Early the next morning, the baby was taken to her mother. The young woman cried out, "My cares are over! I just love the name y'all picked - 'Femally' Jones."

- Lucille Thompson

Royal Richard

As a professional artist, I collected some Richard Petty memorabilia and arranged the items in a framed collage, honoring the driver's 30 years of racing. I was proud of the colorful piece and hoped that one day The King would buy it and display the art in his museum at Level Cross, North Carolina.

The occasion finally arrived. Richard was making an appearance at the Charlotte Motor Speedway. There would be an autograph session for adoring fans around noon. I carefully placed the picture into the car and drove out Highway 29. Wow! I thought I heard trumpets as I approached the Petty Empire. After about 45 minutes shuffling in line, I arrived at the side of The Great One.

"Mr. Petty," I cooed, trying desperately to be heard over the crowd. "I'm an artist and would love to show you a collage I designed praising you and your racing career. I've gathered some mem..."

"Hey there," he interrupted, smiling to an admirer. "Good ta see ya!" He fidgeted in his royal boots. "Ma'am?" he twanged, glancing back at me. He then pulled those ever-present sunglasses down a tad with one hand while reaching to shake another fan's hand.

His regal eyes met mine. "Ma'am," he grinned, "what's a CO-llage?"

- Lucille Thompson

Love is Blind

Although my friend, Inez, lived a sheltered but happy life at an orphanage in a small town in North Carolina, she convinced herself in 1944 that the time had come for her to leave the nest. Over objections that she was too young, Inez, at 16 decided to get married in December.

Henry, her fiance, assured her that he had taken care of all details. He had bought their bus tickets and confirmed their reservations at Hotel Charlotte for three nights, a privilege Inez thought only the wealthy enjoyed.

Their wedding went as planned. Henry and Inez arrived at the Trailways Bus Terminal on Charlotte's Trade Street after dark, then hurried outside to hail a cab. Everything seemed strange---all sorts of people everywhere. Some leaned against the

66

building and stared at her, making her uneasy. *Maybe I am too young to get married,* she thought, as she shivered from the cold. Henry finally stopped a cab, and they jumped in while the driver loaded their bags.

"Where to, sir?" the driver asked.

"Hotel Charlotte, please."

"Hotel Charlotte? Are you sure?"

"Yes, I'm sure," said Henry.

The driver made a quick U-turn and drove into the parking lot directly across the street from the bus terminal. The adjoining structure displayed the neon sign, "Hotel Charlotte."

- Lexie Hill

The British are a Friendly Lot

While on a trip to England, we were on our way back to our hotel from the Tower of London via the underground. I was uncertain as to whether I was heading for the correct train. I stopped at the ticket window. "Pardon me, " I said. "But do I have to change?"

The young man looked up and, with a quick grin, replied, "No, madam, you look lovely."

- Margaret Bates

The Fix-It Man

On a plane trip to Atlanta, I was seated between another man and a mechanic for a race driver near the galley.

While preparing food, a stewardess skidded and slipped on the linoleum, nearly spilling coffee and rolls. She broke a heel off her shoe, but she hobbled on to the rear to serve the back rows. As she returned, the mechanic said, "Here, Honey. Give me your shoe."

She handed it to him, and he opened up his jacket and there was a tool belt. He could have fixed my car with all the stuff in that belt. He took some nails and glue and repaired the shoe in no time flat.

"You must be a minister," she said.

The other guy and I looked at each other.

"Yeah," said the mechanic. "I save heels and souls."

- Bob Welsh

67

Not for Me

As I sat in the dentist's chair during a recent check-up, I was trying to decide whether or not to attempt to ask a question. With a mouthful of tubes, it's very difficult to make intelligible sounds.

Finally, at a point when I felt I could quickly get in a word, I began to tell my hygienist about a problem I had been having with my tongue. She speculated on the cause of the trouble then began to laugh.

"You know," she said, "one of my patients remarked just the other day that she thought it would have been so convenient if God had created us with a zipper at the back of the tongue so we could just remove it when we had to have dental work done."

Smiling down at me the dental assistant added, "I told her I didn't think I would like that. My husband might want me to keep mine out all the time."

- Florine Ledford Olive

Going Sliding

We met at the YWCA's rooming house for single women, Holly House in East Orange, New Jersey. Nadine, whom I had known about six months, approached me with the idea of sharing an apartment. We had many things in common, so I accepted. After settling into a two-bedroom in South Orange, we got down to the business of assigning chores.

On this particular night, it was Nadine's turn to cook dinner. She decided on breaded pork chops. She prepared them with my coaching. We sat down and tried to cut the meat. However, instead of yielding to the knives, both pieces took a slide off our plates, across the table and onto the floor.

Nadine was indignant. "You shouldn't have told me to bread them so much!"

- Harriet Dolin

Rain and Religion

Grandpa and Grandma Spencer were living out in Kansas in the early 1900s near Kansas City. They were members of the Disciples of Christ Church and felt privileged to live right next door to the preacher and his wife.

One night after a long drought, a heavy big-drops rain began at dusk. They glanced out into their neighbors' backyard and saw the Reverend and his helpmate merrily dancing stitch-stark naked in the downpour.

The very next day, Grandpa and Grandma became converted Presbyterians.

- Joy S. Burton

No Handicapped License?

Our neighbor was a brilliant but absent-minded brain surgeon with a large practice and an office in the multi-storied Doctors Building.

One afternoon, his receptionist and patients with appointments waited in vain for his arrival. Finally, the receptionist called his home. "Aren't you coming in this afternoon, Doctor?" she asked. "The patients are waiting."

The physician replied, "Well, I came once, but I couldn't find a parking place."

- Nancy West

Aunt Mattie Belle Carried On

Aunt Mattie Belle heard her own drummer so well that the two of them never gave a thought to the crowd along the parade route. Now that she has marched through the pearly gates, I can see she was a woman (especially a Southern woman) far ahead of her time.

Left a widow with three children during the Great Depression, she promptly honed clerical skills acquired at a pre-World War I business college and informed City Hall of Charlotte that she was ready. Mrs. Mattie Belle Porter was a tall, broad and altogether commanding figure. She rode the bus to the hub of city government for the next 20 years until she was ready to march on.

While enjoying her City Hall career in the tax office, my great aunt pursued another interest which strikes me now as possibly related: selling and buying residences. At the dinner table as a child, I often heard the question, "Where has Mattie Belle moved now?" Whatever the answer, the direction was up.

Over the years, she gradually upgraded from blue-collar Louise Avenue to lace-collar Queens Road, which in Charlotte was about as far as you could move on the social and economic scale.

At one point during this one-woman parade of homes, she owned and lived in an enormous, eight-bedroom house and frugally utilized the space for boarders and roomers. How she managed the dinners, I don't know. Maybe she had the roomers peel the potatoes before she returned home from work.

Even though deeply Southern, born and "brewed" in South Carolina, Mrs. Mattie Belle eventually accepted the reality that her only daughter was married to a Yankee! When it was necessary, she moved her trunk full of large dresses and hats and old property deeds to live in enemy territory, Oreland, Pennsylvania. She granted post-wedding amnesty when the son-in-law there turned out to be "all right."

She refreshed her roots in those refugee years by frequent visits to Charlotte, where she would stay with my mother, her late husband's niece. The two would routinely dine at the now-departed S & W Cafeteria. This custom saved Mother from a lot of cooking, since her visitor required an ample food supply. In family lore, those evenings are remembered because of the pickle. This dignified lady would always top off her meal with a big juicy green dill pickle-to-go. At home, she would contentedly munch all the way through Lawrence Welk.

During one visit, Mattie Belle made an appointment with her former beautician uptown at Belk's Department Store. Mother told her of plans to drive out to the old family home in the rural Steele Creek community that same day. Mattie Belle assured her she would return in time to go. She definitely intended to do that. Thus, when the afternoon wore on with no Mattie Belle, Mother called the beauty shop to inform Mrs. Porter that the car would leave for Steele Creek soon.

Ever cool, this woman received the news when her wet hair was rolled on curlers ready for the dryer (the crucial set after a permanent). "I have to go now," she said and left, large scalp squared off by small curlers. When the bus neared Mother's house on Park Road, the driver Mattie Belle had trained stopped in the middle of the block for the convenience of his curler-topped rider.

She caught the car for Steele Creek and, that night, removed the curlers before take-out pickle time.

Aunt Mattie Belle found "being herself" a satisfying life. She didn't need L'Oreal to tell her she was worth it.

- Nancy West

The Grand Dame

The only person I knew in Augusta, Georgia, when we moved there in 1953, was my sister-in-law Stella and her family. My husband, Seymour, had been there several weeks before I arrived with our two children, Bonnie and Ricky.

Coming from Baltimore couldn't have been more traumatic, because my mother-in-law, Fanny, insisted on driving down after having her driver's license for only two weeks. It's difficult to decide who had more guts: she for her determination or me for taking such a chance with our lives.

Amazingly, we arrived in one piece, except for my shattered nerves. My husband had done me no favor by taking an apartment two doors away from Stella. She was my least favorite person in the whole world. Her tactlessness and sheer meanness had caused me a great deal of aggravation many times through the years.

My mother-in-law, Stella and I were invited to play cards with the Grand Dame of Augusta. A charming, very proper Southern aristocrat, she lived in a lovely old mansion beautifully furnished with priceless antiques. Magnolias scented the air inside and outside her house.

Before our canasta game, we had been served a delicious dessert with coffee and tea in her delicate bone china dishes. Conversation was pleasant, and her cultured Southern drawl was like soft music. Our hostess turned out to be a pretty good card player as well. I really liked her.

Sometime during the evening, she asked me how I was finding Augusta, making small talk as people do when meeting for the first time. "Have you had any problems?" she asked.

Now when a newcomer is talking with someone who has lived in Augusta all her life, complaining about the gigantic brown flying cockroaches would not be in very good taste. So I said, "I'm having a terrible time with pussy ants."

The Grand Dame drew in her breath so fast that her 24-inch strand of real pearls had to readjust themselves on her ample bosom. At first, her eyes widened in disbelief and then closed to slits, as she turned a blotchy red and white. In a strained voice, she repeated, "Pussy ants?"

What had I done? Here I was trying to be on my best behavior, and I had offended this beautiful gracious lady. But what did I say to shock her so? "Well, ya....you see," I stuttered, "pussy aunts are little tiny black ants as opposed to those big black ants we call rain ants."

This didn't help much, and I dug the hole deeper by further explanation. "They come through any little crack from outside and are attracted to food. They're like an army descending on your kitchen."

"Oh...kitchen." She breathed a sigh.

Stella and Mom sat there smirking at my obvious discomfort. In Baltimore, everyone knew they were called pussy ants, and I had no idea they weren't called that all over the United States.

"You *know* we call them pussy ants," I said to my in-laws. I glanced at the Augusta native and back at my sister-in-law. "What do you call them?"

"Ants," declared Stella smugly.

I looked at Mom quizzically.

"Ants," she added.

They knew I was humiliated and embarrassed. And I faced what I had always known --- their resentment of me for having married their favorite son and brother. It delighted them to see me squirm. Of course they knew what pussy ants were. Everybody in Baltimore knew that's what they were called.

What I hadn't realized was that the Grand Dame saw through their denial. She leaned across the table, patted my hand and, after giving Stella and Mom a cold look, said, "In Georgia, we call them piss ants."

That's why she was the Grand Dame and I loved her.

-Harriet Orth

Vic

As the bus crawled toward the base, I reasoned that I might not be going to B-29 training after all, that the dropping of a bomb on Hiroshima could mean the end of the war. I had been told that a group of us would be sent to an accelerated B-29 program to be available for the great invasion of the Japanese homeland. But for now, the Las Vegas Army Air Base, McCarran Field, would be home as we awaited developments.

The barracks was hot---over 100 degrees, and there was a strong scent of melting tar and resin. The central hall was Spartan, scrubbed and unadorned, with little cubicles off each side, for this was officer country, and we were quartered two to a room. I assumed that the left cot was mine, since some

72

musclebound giant, stark naked, was snoring on the other.

The wall studs in our 7'x 9' suite were bare except for a mammoth poster of an ersatz blonde in tights and boots, belt buckle as big as a dinner plate, her oiled muscles rippling like adolescent pythons. She casually held over her head a bar with two weights which looked like the wheels of a small locomotive. At the same time, she smiled happily into the camera displaying a toothy chipmunk grin. A tasteful little tattoo adorned her right thigh. It appeared to be a butterfly roosting on an Easter lily, no doubt a token of some religious symbolism.

The giant awoke, leaped from the cot in one bound, flexed a couple of obscene biceps and said, "Hi! I'm Vic."

I looked up about eight inches into a face as tanned as a GI shoe, with Gary Cooper wrinkles in the corners of his ice blue eyes. His welcoming grin displayed about 76 teeth, all the same size and shape, alike as two rows of Chiclets, every one as white as an angel's nightshirt. The siesta hadn't disturbed the perfectly groomed peroxided hair, styled in a fashion that had not yet migrated to the piney backwoods of Central Florida. I made the mistake of extending my hand, which he promptly crushed, and groaned, "Hello, Vic. I'm Tom Peacock."

"Great. Whole name's Vic Dennis, single silver bar, should be more, hell man, I was a damn hero, just back from pulverizing old Adolf almost single-handed."

During this recital, he was quietly performing and counting a series of effortless straddle jumps, landing as lightly as Mallard down. This was a touch disconcerting, since he was naked as a reindeer, and we were barely 15 inches apart.

"Would home be Southern California, Vic?"

"How'd you know?"

"Just a wild guess."

"You?"

"Florida, Vic. I just spent the summer picking up war weary planes and flying them to storage areas, and I'm ready to head back to Gator country. We're expecting our first baby next month."

"Congratulations."

The conversation lapsed while he pushed both hands against the door frame, muscles pulsing as he did his nude interpretation of Samson among the Philistines. I watched with some apprehension for the collapse of the temple, but he relaxed and the strained timbers snapped back with a crack that reverberated down the hall.

"What you goin' to do when you get out Vic?"

73

"No problem, man. Me and the wife own this little gym between L.A. and the beach, and we're goin' to get rich. Body building is the wave of the future and we're in on the ground floor."

"Your wife, huh?"

"Yep. That's her on the wall."

"You mean that's...?"

"Yeah, man. L.A. County champion three years running in her weight class. She'll have all the old broads down there sweatin' their buns off."

I had the strange feeling that Supergirl might not be the sole source of the old broads' interest.

He continued flexing as I unpacked and made the cot. Just as I finished, he clasped my shoulder in a friendly grip that brought me to my knees, looked carefully around and asked, "What you gonna do for a job?"

"Huh?"

"You know, a job. I'll say it slow. What do you plan to do to occupy yourself on this here air base?"

"I have a job. I'm a pilot."

"Hell, Tom, we're all pilots. Must have 290 on the base, and last time I looked, we only had 18 planes and three of them are down for maintenance. You have to understand. The Colonel believes that idle hands might bring on a revolution or get all of us to playing with ourselves, and everybody, I mean everybody, has to have a job. With the Krauts out of the war and the Nips on their last legs, some people think there is a lack of purpose among the troops. Soooo, the inmates are now running the asylum. For God's sake, don't go near the pool in the middle of the day, or you'll wind up pickin' up cigarette butts."

"Oh come on, Vic. I haven't done that since basic."

"Don't say I didn't warn you."

"What do you do?"

"Run the base gym, of course."

"I should have known. Look, I appreciate your interest. Got any suggestions?"

"Well, I need an assistant at the gym. All we have to do is talk fat Major Henkel into it and you're all set, boy. You can give it a trial run tomorrow."

"Thanks. Just what would I do?"

"Show these weaklings how to condition themselves, of course. Nothing to it."

"Hold it! I've never lifted a weight in my life."

"You won't be able to say that this time tomorrow. Meet me

at 0-800, and bring some shorts and running shoes. Besides, you completed pilot training, so you have to be in some kind of shape." He pulled on some trunks, flipped a towel over his shoulder and whistled his way toward the pool.

The following morning, Vic started me slowly with a few dumbbells and assorted weights but quickly progressed to the real hardware. To my utter surprise, about nine o'clock, I found myself flat on my back. feet in the air, pushing a couple of hundred pounds of cast iron up, then relaxing slowly toward my heaving chest.

Vic was smiling. "Man, you're great with the legs. Where'd you get that leg strength?"

"Teenage paper route. On a bicycle," I wheezed.

"Can't say much for your pecs, though."

"My what?" I asked as my hands moved instinctively toward my pelvis.

"The muscles in the front of your upper chest, stupid."

"Oh."

Seven hours later, I crawled into my cubicle and collapsed. Even my scalp ached. As I lay expiring, Vic sailed in, chinned himself a few times on the door frame, disrobed completely and stood on his head in the corner. As he idly scratched his left shin with his right foot, he said, "Greatest thing in the world. Comes from yoga, and really gets the blood where it ought to be."

"With supreme effort, I propped myself on one elbow and said, "You know, Vic, if you duplicate that pose in the window of your gym, you really ought to attract a whole boat load of old broads, not to mention the cops. Did it ever occur to you that it's hard to carry on a conversation with a guy who's upside down and bare assed? A fellow just can't figure where to look."

"Doesn't bother me. You're too self conscious. The human body is God's supreme handiwork, and I'm just about the supremest example you'll ever see."

I groaned and turned my face to the wall.

About 20 minutes later, he broke the news that an old buddy, nutty as Vic on the subject of conditioning, had just been transferred in, so he was going to have to offer the assistant's job to Tony. Sorry, but there just wouldn't be a place at the gym for me. I signed a long sigh and finally said, "There is a God. And He is good."

"What the hell does that mean?"

"Vic, you just wouldn't understand."

- Tom Peacock

PETS & OTHER LOVEABLE AGGRAVATIONS

A Real Winner

My daughter Gail took Bucky, our aggressive combination chow/shepherd to the Mutt Show at a city park. When she returned, I asked her, "Did Bucky win anything ?"
"Yes, two dogfights."

- Lucy Almand Harrison

Poodle Cut

My dignified father had lost so much of his vision that he didn't enjoy tagging along with Mother in the grocery store, preferring to wait in the automobile instead.

One particularly hot day, he got out to stroll about a bit, and spotted a small white puppy at the open window of a nearby car. He reached in the window and ruffled its fur.

"Hey, whadd'ya think you're doing?" snapped the elderly woman whose curly hairdo had just been thoroughly mussed.

- Bet Ancrum

He-She

One evening, I skidded on a wet kitchen floor, fell and broke my leg. My huge, gorgeous Samoyed dogs responded at once. Kiesh, the male, sat down on my stomach and tenderly licked my face. Natasha, the female, rushed to the front door and barked loudly until my husband (in the front yard) came to my rescue.

I described this to my friend, Ann Black. "Isn't that just like a woman?" I observed. "Natasha took action, ran to get help."

"And isn't that just like a man?" said Ann. "Sees a woman lying on the floor and, right away, jumps on top of her."

- Katherine Kennedy McIntyre

Said What?

My mother, Marie, a gentle Southern lady, never lied. So this story must be true.

She insisted that a large grey cat came up to her back porch and called her by name. "Meowrie," he said.

She looked at him. "Yes?" she answered.

"Meowilk," said the cat.

Mother went to her refrigerator and poured some milk into a saucer. The furry feline had started lapping it when one of my father's large hunting dogs, a Llewellyn setter, spotted the cat and ran up the steps.

The cat exclaimed, "Meowgod!" and disappeared.

- Katherine Kennedy McIntyre

Mistaken Identity

My two sons and I were sightseeing in Williamsburg, Virginia, with our basset hound, Brigitte Bardog, who trotted along with us on a leash. We hastened to pass two men who then followed us closely on the sidewalk. They were obviously fascinated by our pet. One turned to the other and said, "Did you see that German shepherd?"

"That's not a German shepherd," corrected the other. "That's a Pekingese."

- Martha Patterson Spille Hendren

Are You Sure?

Two humanitarian senior adult friends of mine, Mary Frances and her sister, Margaret, have a habit of picking up abandoned dogs and cats and taking them to their veterinarian for complete physicals before they put them up for adoption.

Once, on a country road, they found a pathetic and strange looking dog of mysterious ancestry and breed. They rushed it to the vet for the customary pre-adoption exam.

The caring but puzzled sisters asked the veterinary assistant, "Ray, what kind of dog is this?"

He looked the pooch over thoroughly then replied, "Brown."

- Martha Patterson Spille Hendren

All I Needed Was White Gloves

In June 1971, my husband Bill and I drove to Charleston, South Carolina, to attend a wedding. We took with us our third "child," a teacup poodle. Buffey never weighed over one and a half pounds, and early on, she had trained me to let her be a shoulder dog. Being full-busted, I had a perfect ledge for her rump to rest on.

Late that afternoon, while at the motel dressing for the eight o'clock wedding, we decided we might get hungry before the reception. As soon as Bill left to get us a hamburger and coffee, I thought of Buffey. I opened the door to remind him to bring her a meat patty. Of course, she chose to chase him. I rushed after her, letting the door slam behind me.

After catching her, I looked around and realized my husband was already out of sight, the room door was locked and I had no key.

There I stood in broad daylight in a motel parking lot on one of the busiest corners in Charleston wearing satin slippers, a long half slip, a white bra---and a wiggly fur neck piece.

- Colleen H. Furr

Front Seat Flicka

For our move to Sewanee, Tennessee, we had wedged our 5-month-old daughter's padded bassinet in the back seat of our nearly-perished Oldsmobile. Surrounded by diapers and baby gear, I rode behind my husband Russ. Our beagle, Lila Flicka, shared the front seat with Russ.

Flicka traveled well, sleeping or watching passing scenery as long as the car was in motion. When we stopped, however, she'd go into perpetual motion.

West of Pigeon Forge, we made a multi-purpose stop at a country store and service station. As we were settling back into the car, the friendly female proprietor leaned in the open rear window to take a peek at our wee daughter.

My husband was sliding into the driver's seat and spied Flicka bouncing toward us as if she were going to lick the baby's face. "Girl, you get away from there!" he bellowed. "Don't you dare touch that baby!"

The woman jerked back from the car as though struck by a switch.

- Charlotte R.O. Hallberg

Chessie, the Critic

People say that cats can't talk. Chessie, my gray-and-black-striped tabby, can speak volumes in her own fashion.

She may be sleeping soundly in a ball across the room. But if I sit down to write, she springs to life and, with one leap, is sitting in the middle of my closed notebook. "I don't want you to write. Pay attention to me!" she says.

I answer, "But I need to write this story. Just wait for a few minutes." I slip the notebook out.

Chessie stares closely at me with her green eyes, as if willing me into a trance. I resolutely pick up my pen and make it move across the paper. When I steal a glance, her eyes are slits. But with the slightest move on my part, she begins to stare again. "Aren't you through with that silly stuff yet?" she asks. Her tail uncurls slowly and gives a gentle swish. "Hurry up. I can't wait all day."

When I finally put down the pen, Chessie is all eyes and ears. "Now what?" she wants to know.

"I'm going to read my story out loud. Tell me what you think of it," I say.

As I begin to read, Chessie tilts her head to one side until I finish. She opens her mouth in a wide yawn.

                                                              - Margaret Bates

Now You See It, Now You Don't

"If you want to eat here, no snakes" had been the rule of the house set forth by my friend Lyn, the mother of three teenagers. The youngest, Walt, whom she describes as a "pet freak," had brought home animals of all descriptions. One day he dared bring in a grey rat snake. In a weak moment, she agreed that, if it stayed in an old aquarium with a roof taped on in the basement, she'd tolerate it. She didn't realize that that meant a mouse cage, too, and a mouse-breeding operation to provide food for this most loathed of pets. As the snake grew, so did the size of mice.

Soon after they returned from a brief vacation, someone noticed that the limbless reptile was not in his habitat. Sometimes, it would hibernate under the dirt, but not this time. It was gone. Lyn immediately phoned the local nature museum.

"We get a lot of calls from mothers of teenagers," the spokesman said. "You're worried about whether he'll get in bed with you."

Yes, indeed she was. He assured her that their pet would come up the basement steps only if it wanted to get out to the sun. Snakes prefer warmth and moisture, he said, and theirs would probably be happy in the basement.

Lyn had been away from home for a few days and, upon her return, took some laundry down to the washing machine. Opening the top, she saw her son's dirty clothes already inside and something else that looked suspiciously like a snake. She called its owner downstairs. Promptly.

Walt came and investigated. Muttering something about a shoestring, he derided her for being so squeamish.

Two weeks later, she opened the machine top and saw what she was certain was that cussed thing. Again, Walt---and even her husband---assured her that it was her imagination. Only clothes were in there. Walt worried aloud about her being under a great deal of strain coupled with advancement of age. Hubby, Joe, did turn the machine upside down and examine it for any hole big enough for a snake to slither through. There was none.

The next incident, three weeks later, was even more frightening. There it was, curled around the inside rim of the machine. She carefully closed the top and ran for Joe. Yes, he saw it. He believed! He tried to grab it near the head, but the elusive one hustled to get back between the tub and the outer wall of the machine, and Joe could only catch it near the tail. It stiffened and wedged itself into an irretrievable position.

My exasperated friend got some long scissors, but neither she nor Joe could use them. Theirs was a "politically correct" household, and violence was out of the question.

Bleach! Worth a try. While Joe held the body part as best he could with two hands, Lyn reached around both sides of her protector and held an open bottle of bleach near their captive. After a couple of whiffs, it relaxed, and Joe easily removed it from the hiding place.

Did he sling it out the basement door? Take it to some far-off woods? Nope. While his wife was falling apart, Joe was petting and soothing it. Eventually, he put it back into the aquarium.

Walt, however, traded it for an iguana.

- Margaret G. Bigger

GRANDKIDS & OTHER PEOPLE'S KIDS

Watch Your Pees and Ques

A Sanitation Department inspector was coming to the Winston-Salem school where my fellow-teacher was teaching first grade. So, wanting everything to be in order, she asked the children to be helpful.

To Johnny, she said, "Please be more careful when you use the bathroom."

Quickly he responded, "Mrs. Shore, do you know how hard it is to steer one of these things?"

- Janie Hardy

Watch Out for That Sucker!

My five-year-old nephew Warren was a devoted thumb-sucker. His mother had done everything she could think of to stop his habit. Finally, she came up with the threat, "If you keep sucking that thumb, someday you will blow up and burst."

She was pleased with the effectiveness of her white lie until the day that she and her son were waiting at a street corner for a light to change. A very pregnant woman was standing beside them. Warren looked at the stranger curiously. He walked around one side to get a better glimpse, then glanced up at her shyly and said, "I know what YOU'VE been doing!"

- Selby A. Daniels

A Job Well Done

After tutoring English for a year, I was surprised to read one football player's evaluation of my teaching: "Mrs. Tate is the fairest teacher I had this year, and she taught me everything I no."

- Beth Tate Smith

Unhealthy Wishes

My 4th grade grandson, Danny, is a delight and headache to his teachers in a small Texas town.

Recently, the school principal had a lengthy hospital stay. She would never win a popularity contest, but after all she *was* sick, so every child was required to make a get-well card.

Danny's card had the usual flowery "get well soon" message on the front. Inside he wrote, "'Cause at your age, you could be dead."

- Charlotte R.O. Hallberg

Dessert Anyone?

In the mid '70s, I taught a remedial reading class at a junior high school. One morning, a strong odor of chocolate permeated the classroom. I located the source, one of those huge dollar Hershey bars in the hands of a chubby little blond fellow. Standing over him, I asked, "Don't you know you aren't supposed to eat candy in class?"

He looked up with big innocent eyes and lisped, "What am I 'posed to do with it?"

- Colleen H. Furr

Down Under

In 1938-39, I was teaching high school in Clio, South Carolina. Rembert Pate, a pupil in my homeroom came in one day and told me that all of his grades on his report card that month were submarine grades.

"What do you mean?" I asked.

"They're all under Cs."

- Brice Carson

Define "Hamlet"

I taught English at Columbus High School in Georgia in 1948-49. Several days each week, all senior English classes were required to define spelling words.

One of the words was the common noun, "hamlet."
A girl, Judy Favor, spelled the word correctly. Her definition was "an omelet made of ham."

- Brice Carson

What if...?

Three-year-old Jenni, my grandchild, complained constantly. Finally, her exasperated father threatened, "Do you know what will happen if I take off my belt?"

With wide, innocent eyes, Jenni replied, "Your pants will fall down."

- Clare Barry

Shut Yo' Mouth

My grandsons, Nick, 12 and Tim, 6, had the typical sibling rivalry. They were verbally picking at each other in the family room. "Shut up!" said Nick.

"Shut up!" retorted Tim.

More "shut ups" were exchanged with increasing volume.

Their mother, Bonnie, was at the end of her patience. She said, "If I hear 'shut up' one more time, both of you are going to your room for an hour."

Silence lasted about four minutes. Then Tim spoke up, "Shut DOWN!"

- Paul Jernigan

Why Was That Dress So Pretty?

The church which a friend of mine attends was filled to capacity on Easter Sunday. The minister invited the children in the congregation to come forward for the Children's Sermon. As they gathered around him and sat on the carpet, he greeted many by name.

"Ellen," he said to one 7-year-old, "that's a mighty pretty dress you have on."

In a voice that could be heard all the way to the back pews, she declared, "Yeah, but my mama says it's a bitch to iron."

- Betty Shuford

The Memory Verse

On his return home from Sunday school, Nephew Dan was undergoing a fine-tooth questioning from his mother about what happened in that day's class.

When she got around to asking what the memory verse for the day was, he couldn't remember. In fact, he couldn't even recall what a memory verse was.

"It's a short sentence or two that the teacher keeps repeating and writes on the blackboard."

"Oh yes," said Dan, "I know. It was 'Sit down and be quiet.'"

- Jim Shearouse

Snack Time

Little Robbie, my friend's son, did not eat his lunch one day, so Rooney, his mama wouldn't give him his dessert cookies. She said he could eat the Oreos after his afternoon nap and that he could drink his milk in the refrigerator. She placed the leftover milk in the "fridge" and put the 3-year-old to bed.

Two hours later, Rooney walked into the kitchen to see two little legs sticking out of the barely opened Kelvinator door.

Rob was perched on the second rack, gulping his milk and cookies. Her widened eyes brought the explanation, "I'm drinking my milk in the refrigerator."

- Joy S. Burton

Nose Better

When Jake, my first grandson, was born, I dutifully went to Atlanta to be with him for his first week in the world.

Late in the evening of day four, my daughter Elaine exclaimed, "He can't breathe!"

After carefully checking the problem, I knew this over-protective new mother wasn't going to let me touch the stopped up nose. Panicky, she phoned the doctor, whose call was transferred to the emergency room, since it was after hours. I heard her answer, "No," and knew the question was "Is he turning blue?" After much deliberation, we took Jake to the

86

emergency room for treatment.

The physician probed the dried mucus and cleared Jake's tiny nasal passages. In a soft voice, Doctor Wonderful said, "Older children usually get this stuff out with their fingers."

Elaine sighed. "My husband hasn't taught him to do that yet."

- Sharon McGinn

The Agreement

Recently I took my nephew's two children to breakfast. Both of their parents were busy, so Brian, 6, and Colleen, 4, were my guests. Before going, we had a short conference. There were to be no temper tantrums, and every morsel on their plates were to be eaten. We shook hands and agreed.

We went to an Ohio Tee Jays and ordered. Both behaved very well and ate all their food. While we were waiting for the check, Brian sneezed.

"Do you have a cold?" I asked.

"No, I'm just allergic to adults."

- Helen McDaniel, Ph.D.

The Day of the Rodent

Much to my horror, I discovered an enormous quantity of rat droppings in the dark brown shag rug in our guest bathroom. After my hysteria subsided, I dialed Killo Exterminating Company, demanding immediate service. My 4-year-old nephew, Albert, was visiting us, and I didn't want to send him home with the bubonic plague.

Killo sent two of their finest that afternoon. Upon seeing the mess, both men laughed unrestrainedly. Finally, the younger exterminator, Billy, managed to explain, "Lady, those aren't rat dooky; those are raisins."

Upon interrogation, Albert 'fessed up to the crime. He was somewhat exonerated by his explanation: "Mom told me to mind you and eat all you cooked. But honest, Suz, raisins taste like dog poop."

- Susie Abrams

87

So Who Hid It?

My father had just come home from the hospital after having a double hernia operation. Craig, my nephew, who was 4, and my sister-in-law Phyllis had come over to see us.

Craig was going from room to room before coming back downstairs with a very perplexed look on his face. "Well where is it?" he asked with a great deal of wonder in his voice.

None of us knew what he was talking about. "Where's what?" I asked.

"The new baby!"

We all get a big laugh out of that, but poor Daddy had a hard time suppressing any movement, because he was literally in stitches. It seems that everyone Craig knew who had been in the hospital had brought home a baby.

- Harriet Orth

Putting Up a False Front

When my friend Robbye was young, her family lived in Memphis, Tennessee, in the mid-'40s. One evening, they were entertaining her father's colleagues, airline pilots, and their wives.

The adults were conversing in the living room when Robbye's 3-year-old brother, Mike, toddled into the room. "Mama, can I play telephone with these?" One of his mother's flesh-colored foam rubber falsies hung from his ear. The nipple of the other one drooped from his mouth.

- Margaret G. Bigger

What Mess?

Fellow freelance writer E. J. McGee worried about her daughter's messy habits when she prepared her to go to college. "How will you be able to live with another girl in a small room, if you can't even keep this one picked up?" she asked Emme repeatedly.

"I'll just get one that's like me," Emme would reply.

Finally, the big day came. Just before their early morning departure for the state university, Emme's father made one final check of her room to make sure she hadn't forgotten anything.

88

He was aghast to see the mess. Nothing had changed!

"Emme, get up here and clean up this room!" he yelled.

As she ambled in and surveyed the scene, she asked, "Do I have to make up my bed?"

- Margaret G. Bigger

Who's Who?

Bobby's parents were friends of ours in the '50s. Everyone thought Bobby's nickname for his father was cute. Just learning to talk, he loved the attention he got whenever he used it.

But father John wasn't amused when he took his son grocery shopping. Customers and clerks stared when the little fellow trailed his father up one aisle and down the next calling, "Mama, Mama!"

- Nancy West

Too Tiny

My friend's family was rather spread out in age, so her youngest was scarcely old enough to be the flower girl in her eldest daughter's wedding.

Baby Ann, excited by her dress and basket, performed beautifully at the rehearsal. Then came the ceremony.

The Wedding March sounded, and the procession began. As the bride came down the aisle, she was preceded by a rising titter. The 3-year-old hadn't realized the church would be full of people. The father of the bride clumped bravely along with his oldest daughter on his arm and his baby daughter clamped firmly around his other leg.

- Katherine McAdams

Look Out!

At a remote end of the Okefenokee Swamp, my Girl Scout adventure troop paddled, sang, laughed and scared away all wildlife for miles around. On this three-day trip, we would never set foot on dry land. At the end of a day's paddle, we would seek a platform for camping.

When the sun burned hotter, they asked if they could take their shirts off. A leader for many years, I thought, why not? We are the only ones who could possibly be here, for just one group is allowed in the area at a time. Not only that, we could have heard the Park Ranger coming in his little putt-putt boat from a mile away.

Off came most shirts, and we had a glorious morning, winding around the cypress trees and looking for alligators. I had forgotten one important thing. As we came around a bend, we suddenly came face-to-face with a Boy Scout troop on the way out from the campsite we were heading toward.

The girls shrieked, dived for their shirts, giggled and moved on loudly. The boys, who were younger, looked straight ahead with stony, stunned faces and stroked silently past us. It would appear they had not even noticed our encounter.

Some months later, at a meeting of Boy Scout and Girl Scout leaders, I repeated my tale again for the tenth time and concluded with "I guess I will always enjoy telling that story."

An older Boy Scout leader leaned back and said, "Katherine, you go on telling your story, but I do wish you could hear the stories those Boy Scouts are telling."

- Katherine McAdams

Pool Hopping

"Bob, wake up!" My wife, Marlis shook me. "There's someone outside the window."

I crept up to the open window, while Marlis was saying she would call the police. I waved her off of the notion, as I heard several male voices, one of them whispering, "Kathy, Kathy!"

They had the wrong window. Our daughter, Kathy and her friend, Susan, were sleeping in another bedroom. I raised my voice several octaves, and mimicking Kathy, said, "Yes?"

"It's me, Bobby. Is Susan in there?"

"Yes," I said. "What are you doing?"

"We're all out here in our underwear. And we're pool hopping."

"Shame on you, Bobby," I said, in my Kathy-voice.

"Come on out!"

"Okay, we'll be right there," I said. I told Marlis to count to ten and then turn on the outside lights.

It was a hot moonlit night, and I had been sleeping in my

underwear. As the lights snapped on, I jumped out the front door yelling. "Here we are Bobby, in our underwear!"

Four boys flew like quail.

- Bob Welsh

Who Did Grandpa Shoot?

We hate guns! We wouldn't have one in the house, but we love our shoot-out hole.

A shoot-out hole? The 200-year-old log cabin in our back yard has one. It is an opening concealed by a short piece of log which was never chinked in. Its name explains its purpose.

A group of preschool children visited us because of their love for Smokey Bear, that symbol of conservation in a Ranger hat. We honored Smokey by celebrating trees: raked leaves for jumping, red apples for munching, loft ladder for climbing, sawdust clay for modeling and a buggy seat for bouncing.

The shoot-out hole was, of course, the biggest hit. My dear husband Leonard lifted each child high enough to peek through the opening from the inside and the outside.

We were weary but satisfied that their visit had reinforced the bear's message, "Don't play with matches!"

But back at school, one little boy reported, "I learned that Mr. Harrison shot Smokey Bear through the shoot-out hole."

- Lucy Almand Harrison

A Job Worth Doing . . .

My strapping teenage grandson was leaning against the car, idly twanging the antenna, as I reached into the trunk for the heavy bags of groceries. Having second thoughts, I sarcastically said, "Wait a minute, Douglas - *you* take the groceries in the house for *me*, and *I'll* twiddle the aerial for *you*."

Douglas grinned and promptly gathered up the groceries, and I took his place twiddling the antenna. As he headed for the door, he turned around, studied me briefly and remarked archly, "You're not doing it right, Grandmother."

- Bet Ancrum

91

JUST HOW SEXY CAN A SENIOR CITIZEN BE?

Auction Action

For my husband Russ and me, auctions are great spectator sports. Dreams cost nothing.

At one in Nacogdoches, Texas, a long low shed held saddles, spurs, chaps and a huge enameled coffee pot. On a handmade table was what I wanted, needed, must have: a shiny silver tea service! My desire for it was making me pant.

Eyes closed, I nuzzled over to Russ, clasped his hand and said in a soft tone that promised other things from me in return, "Oh what I'd give - anything - to have that silver service."

Beneath my half-opened lids, I saw not khakis and Keds but greasy jeans and heeled boots. A dry, crackly Texan voice said, "I sure can't afford that metal, but maybe I could buy you a Co-cola."

- Charlotte R.O. Hallberg

Rx: Sex

When my parents were in their 80s, Mother read aloud an article that said sex often serves as an analgesic for arthritis.

"So," she coyly concluded to Dad, "maybe we ought to go back to some of our old habits, Ernest!"

Dad hurumphed, "I 'druther take Tylenol."

- Bet Ancrum

You Can't Go Home Again

My parents retired to the North Carolina mountains, where they had summered many years previously. Wending her way

93

slowly up US 176 one day, Mother saw two overalled men standing beside a weary pickup truck. Thinking she recognized one as the local stonemason, Hix Hill, she waved out the window to them, calling gaily, "Hi, Hix!"

The indignant mountaineers were total strangers.

- Bet Ancrum

Know Your Endorser

On their first Saturday back in the North Carolina mountains where she and Daddy had owned a summer home 15 years earlier, Mother sought to cash a check. She tried her old pharmacy, only to find a new young druggist who refused to take a stranger's check.

Just then Mrs. Boys entered the store, and Mother re-introduced herself to her friend from the past. Mrs. Boys offered to vouch for her, and the reluctant druggist counted out five twenties into Mother's palm.

He paled visibly, however, at the ladies' cordial parting from one another:

"Thank you ever so much, Miriam."

"It's *Muriel*."

- Bet Ancrum

Too Many Funerals

When my sister entered a funeral parlor to bid farewell to the deceased, she first greeted the mourners. A friendly person, she kissed many of the women, as they embraced. Upon finally reaching the casket, she discovered it held a stranger---like the ones she'd just kissed.

- Clare Barry

Mission Accomplished

It's a major decision to move into a retirement community. My friend Eva Satterfield was most helpful.

"You and I are packrats," she said. "Our houses are full. We save everything. I have a plan for you. Move into Merrywood. Your family will help you clear out your house. After they dispose of everything, they will take care of any repairs needed. Then they'll probably paint it. It's at this point, Katherine, that you move back in."

- Katherine Kennedy McIntyre

Oops!

When my mother met her elderly Sunday school teacher while shopping with a friend, the teacher uttered these words of apology, "Dears I think of each of you as one of my dearest friends, but at this moment, I can't think of either of your names."

- Beth Tate Smith

Not Exactly a Pig in a Poke

Store managers love to hire seniors like me who display a spirit of friendliness to shoppers.

One day, when the computer scanner malfunctioned to show that the customer was due $827.50 in change, I politely asked her, "Would you like your change in a paper or plastic bag?"

- Bill Prall

In Case of Medical Emergency

On a recent trip to the Canadian Rockies, we met a lady we will call Barbara who had a fantastic outlook on life, despite being 80+ in years. When she learned that two doctors were in our group, one a psychiatrist, the other a gynecologist, she was elated. "Great!" she said. "This week, if I get pregnant or lose my mind, I'll be in good company."

- Bill Prall

Hello, Who's There?

After learning that the person I wished to speak with was out of his office, I was leaving my number with his secretary for a return call.

"Do you have an answering machine?" the secretary asked.

"No, thank goodness!" I answered vehemently.

"But they *are* useful from time to time," was her gentle comment.

"Not for me," I replied. "I'm 83, and there's hardly anyone left to call me but God. When THAT one comes, I surely don't want to receive it second-hand!"

- Nancy Helms

Confined in Retirement

After his retirement in the mid-'40s from the UNC faculty, a friend was not in when a former student stopped by his home in Chapel Hill.

"I'm sorry, son, he isn't here," our friend's wife said grimly. "I have no idea when he'll be back."

"I have to leave in two hours. Do you know where I can find him?" asked the caller.

"Why yes. He's in the iron lung."

"Oh!" said the concerned visitor. "Which hospital is he in? Perhaps I can run by to see him for a moment."

"He's not in the hospital, son. He's at The Shack, the beer parlor down by City Hall. The old men in town think they can't live outside it."

- Nancy Helms

This Tooth Shall Pass

Recently, my dentist was attempting to put a gold crown on one of my teeth, when the crown slipped and---whoops!---went right down my throat.

He and I both knew it was worth several hundred dollars and just had to be recovered. He gave me instructions, as if I didn't know, how to go about finding it.

That was Wednesday, and after diligent searching and inspections, I still had not found it by the next Sunday.

That afternoon, I had to bend double to look under a car seat for an article I'd put there. The effort made me cough vigorously. To my surprise, something popped out of my mouth. After all my searches in vain, could it be...? *This time* it really

96

was! But I still think it's amazing how a kernel of corn can resemble a gold crown.

- Jim Shearouse

Sudden Death

I visited my older sister, Margaret, at the nursing home after a long absence.

"Hello, Faison," she said. "I thought you were dead."

"No," I responded, "just brain dead."

"I was especially sad to hear about your death," she continued, ignoring my response. "You were the brightest member of the family."

"That makes me the youngest horse in a glue factory."

- Faison Barnes

Taking Care of the Kiddies

As my husband was expounding at his 70th birthday party, "Fellow septuagenarians...," one of his teachers from the local community college entered, accompanied by a small shapely young girl.

This nice-looking man in his 50s had mentioned to my husband that he might bring his 13-year-old daughter. Of course, I had begun to plot a romance between my grandson and his daughter. Since our guests needed attention, we led them to the beverage counter and inquired of him whether he preferred red or white. Chattily, I turned to the girl and said, "I know your daddy doesn't permit you to drink wine. Would you like soda or juice?"

Her eyes shot fire, and her mouth twisted as she answered, "Well, actually, he's my boyfriend, and I prefer red!"

- Hope Schene

Trouble's Brewing

My friends Pearl and Harry had been married for over 30 years. One day, Pearl confided to me that Harry was acting very strange, distant and---well, just not himself. "He spends a lot of time upstairs in his office and calls someone every night from there and talks at length," she told me worriedly.

"How can he have an affair over the phone?" I marveled.

"He isn't home all the time you know," she said.

Pearl was much too polite to "listen in." Besides, the suspect might hear the click. She racked her brain for a way to corner him. One day, her answer came. She would be patient.

That night, Harry finished in his office as usual around 9 p.m. after his long phone call and went to take a shower. Pearl bravely went up to the office and stood poised over the phone. She knew exactly what to do. Her hands trembled as she picked up the telephone and pressed REDIAL.

"Hello," her mother-in-law answered.

- Sharon McGinn

Auntie

Auntie suffered terribly with aches, pains and stiffness. She had arthritis and osteoporosis, with all the general lumbago complaints. Our aunt was barely comfortable, not well-to-do. After years of complaining, praying and avoiding expensive physicians, her eyes caught some advertisements in the Charlotte telephone book's Yellow Pages---finally, someone she could go to who would manipulate those sore muscles and soothe those aching bones. Forget those regular doctors, here were practitioners who could give her some relief. And the ads showed that most were out near the airport, easy to locate.

Auntie sped her rusty faded green 1980 Chevrolet toward the airport, her gnarled hands clutching the steering wheel. She pulled up at the Yellow Page address and rushed to the entrance. Imagine her shock when a very young pretty girl with white-blond hair opened the mobile home door, scantily clad in red and white boudoir lingerie!

Auntie left in a bigger hurry than she came.

- Joy S. Burton

Early Retirement - Very Early

Moving two households of furniture to one house was exhausting. But it was worth it, because the blending was due to a joyous second marriage.

After unpacking enough pots, pans and dishes for supper, I said to my new husband, "Honey, I've found a way we can, with just one more move, never have to move again!"

He looked interested, so I explained, "Mother and I visited the Methodist Home this afternoon. Not only do they have large buildings for those who need various levels of care, but people can build cottages on the grounds. If we put one on the very edge of the property, by the time we turn 65, we would already be retired! And we'd never have to move again!"

My husband said nothing. But my new "cool" 14-year-old stepson said, "Yeah, great! When the guys at school ask me where I live, I can say, 'The Old Folks Home'!"

- Lucy Almand Harrison

Wake Up Call

It was 6 a.m., when my friend, Inez, a lovely lady in her senior years, shook her sleeping husband and said, "Honey, wake up. There's something I need to tell you!"

"What is it?" he murmured.

"I know you'll be mad with me."

"OK, what is it?" he answered sharply.

"See you're already mad with me."

"No, I'm not mad with you. I just woke up, for goodness sake!"

"But I know you're going to be mad with me when I tell you."

"What did you do?" he shouted.

Inez waited a moment, then said softly, "I can't tell you."

"I *am* mad with you now."

"The car has been running all night," she blurted out.

He sighed. "How long?"

"Since three o'clock yesterday afternoon 'til six this morning. I went out to get the paper and noticed smoke coming out of the exhaust and realized I had left the car running."

There was a long pause before he asked, "How much gas did you have in the car?"

"A fourth of a tank," Inez said.

Her husband smiled. "We really got good gas mileage, didn't we, Honey?"

- Lexie Hill

Daddy Hangs 10

When Daddy reached 73, we again heard his lament. There were two things he had never experienced: parachuting out of a plane and white-water rafting.

Mother said he had no business jumping out of a plane. If man were meant to fly, he would be covered with feathers and sport a beak. And if he wanted to experience white water, throw a cup of Joy in the bath water and splash away.

A day came when everyone knew something was up. Daddy always gets a quirk in his eyebrow when he knows something the rest of us don't know and is laughing inside. He had that look at dinner.

The raft left the banks of the New River at daybreak on a splendid Saturday morning with nine hale and hearty young people including my sister Barb and Daddy.

"Sit across from me, Daddy," Barbara said, as they began their adventure.

The water barely rippled, as the raft smoothly glided down the river. The guide pointed out interesting landmarks, while the crew paddled leisurely and waved gaily to those in other rafts nearby.

However, the tranquility soon disappeared along with the raft directly in front of them. One minute it was there, and the next it seemed to be swallowed by a frothy whirlwind. Daddy said later that his only thought was, it's too late to back out now.

"Paddle to the left!" shouted the guide, and paddles hit the water like blades of a mixer.

One side of the raft sank about four feet, which raised the other side a corresponding distance. Daddy shot into the air as if he'd been drop kicked. He hit the water with arms and legs flailing, sank briefly and came up laughing.

"Daddy are you all right?" Barb screamed.

He assured everyone he was fine, as they dragged him back in. He settled in another area of the raft between two burly fellows, and everyone resumed paddling.

After a time, the ride smoothed out, and a few jokes were made about Daddy's sailing. The calm interlude was short-lived, though, as rafts ahead began their disappearing acts and the guide began shouting instructions. "Paddle to the left, now the right!"

Daddy went sailing out again.

"Frank, are you all right?" asked Barb, who by this time

had dispensed with calling him Daddy.

After reeling him in a second time, the guide sat him amidships and told him to hold on to a rope that was so small, it probably wouldn't have held a kitten. And there he teetered for the remainder of the trip with the exception of the picture-taking ritual.

The cost of the trip included a picture of one's raft as it battled the rapids. When they rounded a bend, the guide told everyone to smile for the cameraman stationed on the bank. But about that time, they hit another big gully. Barb was thrown forward into the bottom of the raft, and Daddy toppled over on top of her.

"Get off me, Frank!" she yelled.

The picture reveals the guide, eight hale and hearty young people, a tangle of arms and legs and a foot which Barb says is hers.

But the best thing is that Daddy got to experience the thrill of parachuting after all.

- Jeannine Southers

Taking Stock

You know you're on a streetcar ride down the other side of that proverbial hill when:

You look at your reflection in a mirror or store window and wonder who on earth that elderly person is.

It takes at least four rings to get out of your chair to answer the phone.

You talk for 20 minutes to another oldtimer about your aches and pains.

Your hair becomes see-through, and the exposed scalp looks as pink as a baby's bottom.

You see someone approaching who is really an old friend, but the name doesn't surface until you say goodbye.

You make a note of your own phone number somewhere for fear you won't be able to recall it when you need it.

You realize that potty training is not necessarily forever.

It takes a whole lot more than a cup of coffee to get you started in the morning - like a blast from the teenager's car radio down the street.

Your skin either decides to toughen, sag or wrinkle in places for the whole world to see.

Your eyesight is a bit dimmer, your hearing a bit less keen, but your tongue seems to be loose at both ends.

Your children are now at the age when you first began to feel old.

You dare not change your daily routine lest you forget to do something vitally important, like checking to see if your shoes match.

Well-meaning friends begin to try to interest you in a retirement home, and you know you should listen but say to yourself, "No way! Those places are for *old* people!"

A book labeled "explicit sex" doesn't pique your interest - just exhausts you to think about it.

You compare today's cost of living with "the good old days." Of course, then there were few things to do, fewer places to go, not much to buy and precious little to buy it with.

You mention a literary classic to your grandchildren, and they don't have the vaguest notion what you are talking about.

You're no longer asked if you are old enough to qualify for senior citizens' fares.

You look at what we wore in the '20s and '30s and realize they are now period costumes.

It takes a month to recover after your children and grand-children have been home for a visit.

Twenty minutes of exercise nearly puts you to bed.

You remember clearly what happened when you were 6, but you can't recall whether you took your medication after breakfast this morning.

The younger generation seems to be attired either in outer space garb or cast-offs of sharecroppers.

The very thought of wearing high heels makes you dizzy.

Your doctor's diagnosis is usually, "You're no spring chicken, you know," which means he hasn't the faintest clue what is wrong.

You can't remember how much you weighed when you got married or what color your hair was.

Your eye shadow gets lost in folds of skin, and your nail polish clashes with your liver spots.

You can remember when living together meant you had been down the aisle, not just for a drive around the block.

Your children are talking about technology you've never heard of just when you thought you knew everything.

You don't dare bend over 'til you've looked around to see if there's something or someone nearby to help you back up.

Those strict Victorian manners and morals begin to look

better and better to you.

Everything you really like to eat either keeps you awake, gives you heartburn, causes a stomach ache, or some three-initialed agency declares it unsafe.

You find little notes all over the house reminding you what to do next or what you forgot to do yesterday.

But the good news is that, thankfully, you at least are still on that nostalgic streetcar ride, and you haven't reached the bottom of that hill yet!

- Florine Ledford Olive

I'm So Old, I Can Remember When . . .

* Getting "bombed" was what happened to England during the blitz, getting "potted" was for geraniums, "grass" was to spread a picnic cloth on, "hay" was for hayrides, and you made snowballs from "snow."

* "Gay" meant happy, "swell" was good and a "fag" was a cigarette.

* Men and boys were ashamed to wear jeans; women and girls rarely ever wore them.

* Females were embarrassed by wrinkled or faded clothes.

* A long distance call meant a death in the family, and party lines weren't always fun and games---but were cheaper (unlike call-interrupt programs we now *pay* for).

* Mailboxes were olive drab, telephone company trucks were dark green and Lucky Strike green went to war, but hospital personnel wore white and chalkboards were black.

* Bank employees and business people dressed dignified---even on Fridays.

* Girls wouldn't let their underwear show, and they always wore it.

* "Hubba, hubba!" was the spoken equivalent of a wolf whistle---and both were considered compliments.

* Turkey brought to mind Thanksgiving; bunny, Easter.

* Rattails were attached to rats, crawdads didn't wear baseball caps and hornets didn't work in beehives, cheered on by honeybees.

* Ms. was the abbreviation for misspelled.

* And thongs went between the *toes*.

- A compilation

103

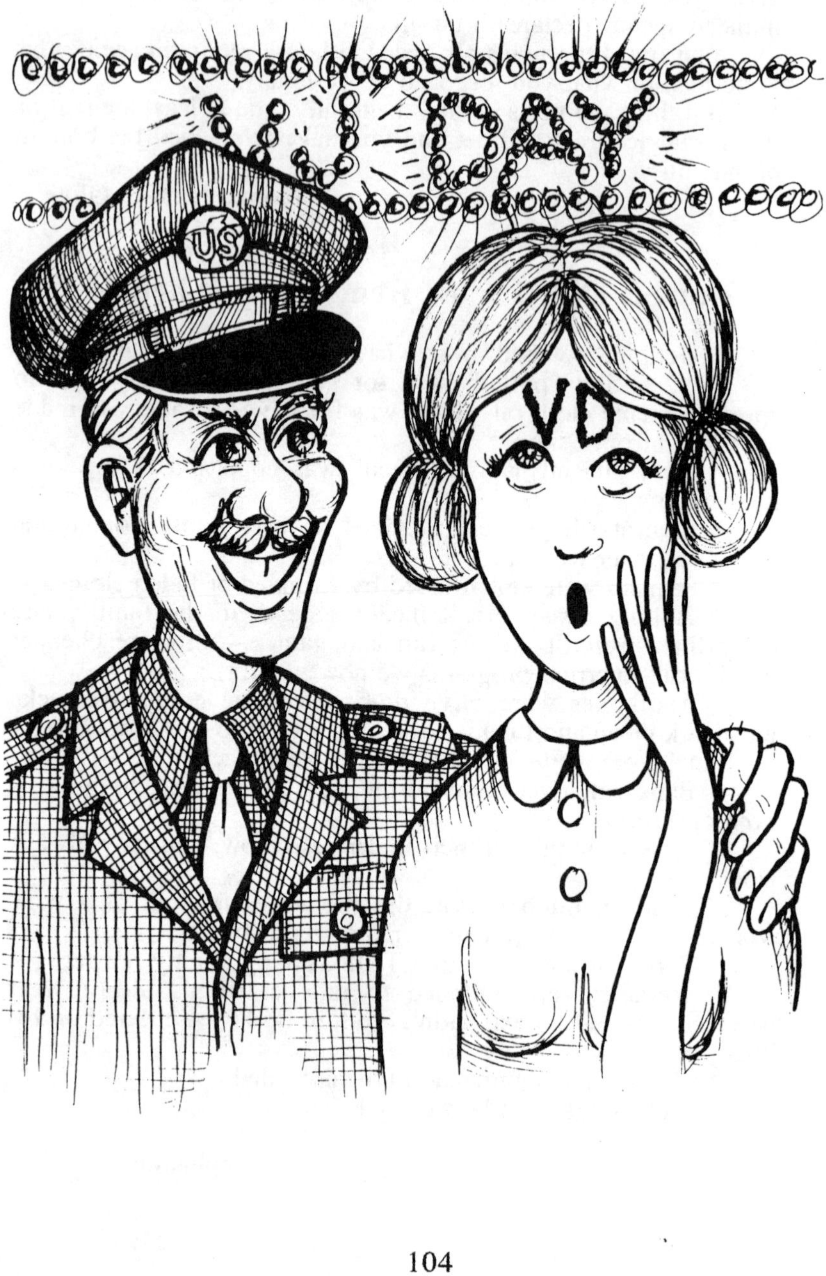
VJ DAY
US
VD

THE LIGHTER SIDE OF HISTORY

The Great Depression

A Guilty Pleasure

My mother said things were so tight in Clearwater, Florida, during the Depression, that their only recreation was a Saturday night drive to the dairy store, where they watched me eat a nickel ice cream cone.

I accepted this mild guilt trip, until I became an adult and realized that we always had an automobile and gas to go in it.

- Katherine McAdams

Depression Delight

Mississippi, I believe, was hardest hit by the Great Depression, even though Eudora Welty claims that the state of Mississippi is in a continual depression. During that darkest, deepest dreariest time in the 1930s, my wonderful father lost his business in Clarksdale, along with a whopping big salary and our car. He saved only our house with two mortgages on it.

Candy and sweets were so rare then, that a tiny bag of gumdrops seemed almost like a Roman banquet to us children.

About that time, a relative had given Mother a box of Whitman's Sampler chocolates, her favorite. From past experience, she knew that, if she left the box of chocolates in our presence, she'd be lucky to get a single piece. She told us we could select *only one* bonbon, just *one*. We chose carefully and then she informed us she was going to hide the Sampler.

We wondered where it was but couldn't find it until she made biscuits one night for supper. When she preheated the oven, we smelled scorched cardboard and burned chocolates.

- Martha Patterson Spille Hendren

Eight is Enough

In 1935, during the Great Depression, our government instituted a program to provide work for the needy. Unemployed men in our rural area of North Carolina signed up for this program called Works Project Administration, better known as W.P.A. Local farmers dubbed W.P.A. as "We Piddle Around."

I remember watching trucks filled with men, equipment and always a portable toilet go by our farm. These men built bridges, public buildings and parks and repaired roads. They even did landscaping.

A prominent lawyer in our area arranged for these workers to maintain his spacious lawn for the summer. Every Thursday, neighbors watched as eight men unloaded two lawn mowers and two outhouses from the truck.

One neighbor, amazed at all the commotion, asked the head man of the crew, "Sir, why does it take *eight* men with only two lawn mowers to mow the lawn?"

"Why that's simple," he said. "There's two a-comin,' two a-goin,' two a-sittin' and two a -mowin.' That's *eight,* ain't it?"

Yep, the more things change, the more they remain the same.

- Lexie Hill

Outhouse or Hothouse?

It's just not true: that you can get used to anything. I *never* got used to our outhouse. Maybe I should have been grateful our family had one; some families didn't. Even in the early '30s in rural North Carolina, those people went behind the barn and shared space with the cows.

Our outhouse was a three-holer with a Sears Roebuck catalog (for looking and wiping), and I hated it. I could see the spider webs and the spiders under the cut-out hole, just where I sat. I always thought, *What if a spider bit my bottom?* and *What if I fell in?*

As soon as the new catalog came in the mail, Mama banished it to the outhouse because, she said, "You spend entirely too much time looking and begging when you should be doing your homework." What Mama didn't know was that the Sears Roebuck catalog allowed me to push my fear and hatred of the outhouse out of my mind as I browsed its pages of stuff I had never seen before.

As the big day approached, the day my cousin Mabel, a city girl, was coming to visit, I was giddy with anticipation. I helped Mama clean the house so it was spic and span and swept the yard. Then I headed for the outhouse. I scrubbed the seats, made sure the spiders were out of the holes and put a box of baking soda in the corner behind one of the seats. I knew Mabel had a bathroom in her house, and I wondered how in the world she was going to be able to use this thing.

Finally the day came. Her father was driving a sleek new Model A. Maybe they wouldn't see Daddy's old Model T under the shed of the barn where it rested because, during the worst of the Depression, Daddy didn't have money to buy gas.

Mama had cooked all the day before, and she laid out quite a spread for dinner: chicken, country ham, vegetables from the garden, sweet potato pie and chocolate cake. I bet Mabel's parents never had a dinner like this!

After dinner, all the grown folks were sitting in the yard under the shade of the big oak tree talking. Mabel and I were jumping rope, when we heard someone yell to my father, "Mr. Silas, Mr. Silas!" Everyone looked toward the sound, and we saw Henry Gaye, our neighbor who lived across the street on a hill, looking down at us. He cupped his hands around his mouth and shouted, "Mr. Silas, your sh..t house is on fire!"

I was so embarrassed I could die! *What will Mabel and her parents think of us now?*

Daddy jumped up, the rest of us following, and ran to the blazing outhouse. My brother, playing with matches, had set the Sears Roebuck on fire! Everyone stood around, hushed, and watched it burn.

Right then, I didn't care about what Mabel or anyone else was thinking. I was glad the outhouse was burning down. My glee suddenly turned to grief--- *No! Oh no! my Sears Roebuck is burning with it!*

                                                    - Lexie Hill

Cree

From my playhouse window, I could see her---Cree, with all her cats, cats of all kinds, running wild and free. She lived across the fence in an unpainted shack behind a pale green colonial. The shack may have been a large woodshed at one time.

If you asked Cree her age, she would say, "Steppin' outa sebenty nine; steppin' into eighty."

And if you asked, "How many cats?" she would say, "Thuty-nine."

My father said it seemed to him she looked exactly the same when he was a little boy. He thought her name may have come from "Creole."

Nancy Zemp, owner of the colonial, wanted Cree to leave. She said the cats were too much. "But I can't make her go," she explained. "If I did, she would travel up and down the street, singing and telling everybody I threw her out. I wouldn't have a friend left in this town."

Cree earned money singing spirituals in a cracked, quavering voice. Her small body ambled everywhere. She would stand, arms akimbo, wizened head leaning to one side, hand on hip, dark face a cobweb of wrinkles, foot tapping the earth.

"Swang low, sweet cha-yu-ut,
  Coming for to ca' me hum-m-m."

People dropped money into the hat she passed around. She always announced that it was for her church, but privately admitted she kept it in her mattress.

She often climbed the fence and serenaded my friends and me. We adored her and contributed all the nickels and dimes we could get together.

One day, when she saw a young man riding horseback with me, she beckoned for me to come to the fence. "Marry him, Sugar Pie," she whispered in my ear. "His family own half the land in the county."

Moultrie Burns was a community leader, president of the local Rotary Club, a successful businessman. He was concerned about Cree.

"Cree," he told her, "your friends worry about you. If you keep your money in your mattress, someone may come in the night, knock you over the head and rob you. If you put your money in our bank, where I keep mine, it will be safe. You too."

"Thank you, Mr. Moultrie. I'll surely do that, first thing in the morning. Thank you, sir."

The Great Depression struck. Our bank failed. The money I had saved, dollar by dollar, was gone. Everybody was broke.

My father had heard about Cree's money. He went to see her. "How can we help, Cree? There was no way anybody could know this would happen. I'm so sorry about your money."

Cree bowed her head, then raised it and looked straight into his eyes. Her wrinkled face shaped into a crooked smile. "Don't you worry, Captain. I knew my money was safer in my mattress. I got it all."

She was probably the only person in Camden, South Carolina, with cash intact. At the wedding of a young white woman whom she had cared for as a child, Cree handed her a hundred dollars for a wedding present.

Looking back, I think Cree learned from her cats how to land on her feet. Or maybe they learned it from her. She was a survivor.

She finally began to trust in banks. She deposited all her earnings into a savings account and collected interest. This impressed her so much that she wrote a will and left all her money to Mr. Henry Carrison, president of the Bank of Camden, "because he took such good care of it."

- Katherine Kennedy McIntyre

Prohibition

The Decanter

One day, when I was about 8 years old, I overheard a conversation between my parents in Camden, South Carolina.

"Marie, I think the cook has been tippling. Look at my decanter. The apricot liqueur is low; the creme de menthe almost gone."

My mother was a teetotaler. But she was also an artist, and she loved the decanter. It was cut-glass, divided four ways---creme de menthe, cherry, apricot and lemon. She hesitated a long moment. "Rob," she finally said, "liqueur is not like whiskey." She made a face like the one she wore when she gave us castor oil.

"Marie, you don't mean you've been drinking?"

"Rob, liqueur is not like whiskey." She made the face again.

My father's smile was like a thousand balloons let loose. "No, Marie," he answered. "No, it's not like whiskey. Just 90 proof, that's all. Just 90 proof."

- Katherine Kennedy McIntyre

Macho German

I may never have gotten here, if it were not for my grandfather's still. He did not live in the backwoods or up in the hills. His still was in an apartment in an 83rd Street brownstone in Yorkville, the German section of New York City.

My grandfather, Peter Krupp, was a socialist. He immigrated from Germany after the failure of the socialist revolution there (also to avoid the draft). As soon as he became a citizen, he voted regularly for the Socialist Party candidates, Eugene Debs and Norman Thomas. He did not agree with the Prohibition law. He believed a man had a right to his schnapps. We do not know how he learned the process or who built the all-copper still for him. A cabinetmaker, he had a lot of friends in the construction business.

Peter had two sons and a daughter. He was very protective of the girl, and suitors were carefully scrutinized. Peter was a powerful man. He once smashed the "hit the bell" machine at Coney Island by slamming it so hard.

My father, Bill Orth, was not athletic, although he belonged to a German gymnastic club. That was where he met my mother. He was an accountant, a profession slightly suspect by Peter. Dad had to prove himself when he came courting my mother. Peter offered him some of the schnapps, dripped directly from the still (about 150 proof, raw and unaged). My father quaffed it down like water without a cough. That proved he was a real man. Bill became a favorite of Peter's, much preferred over the sissified zither teacher who was in competition.

Who knows? If it were not for that still, I might be more musically inclined today.

- Bill Orth

Never on Sunday

Back in the '50s, when South Carolina was a dry state, Charleston completely ignored the liquor laws (except when the grand jury was in session, some say). They had cocktails listed on the menu in restaurants.

However, I was visiting there one Sunday with some friends. At a famous seafood restaurant, two of us picked a cocktail from the dinner menu. A couple of others asked for beer.

"Sorry, we can't serve beer on Sunday," the waiter informed us. He explained that beer and wine were legal if you had a license, but you could lose your license if you sold them on Sunday.

"What about those cocktails we ordered?" we asked.

"Oh, that's liquor. It's illegal all the time, so it doesn't make any difference on Sunday."

- Bill Orth

World War II

Crime Doesn't Pay

My former husband, Seymour Goodman, joined the service with his boyhood friend, Dave Cohen. They went through boot camp at Bainbridge, Maryland, together and somehow survived.

Seymour, coming from a religious Jewish home, had never eaten anything but Kosher food. Every time they went to the mess hall, he would get nauseated and give his meal to Dave. Dave grew pleasingly plump, and Seymour darn near died from starvation.

Being in the Navy, they had to pass a swimming test before they graduated. Seymour was an excellent swimmer, having spent the summers on the Severn River in Maryland at their shore house. Dave, on the other hand, could barely dog-paddle.

Seymour dived into the pool and passed his test without any hitches. But the water was freezing, and he was afraid Dave would drown. They switched dogtags, and Seymour took the test for his friend.

When they got back to their bunks, Dave thanked Seymour profusely for standing in for him. Seymour handed him his tags. "No problem, buddy. You are now a swimming instructor."

- Harriet Orth

Raid on Romance

My sister married her soldier around 1942 in Rutherford, New Jersey. I was the flower girl.

After the at-home wedding ceremony, the guests slowly mingled. Mom began her rounds with the hors d'oeuvres, and Dad uncorked the first bottle of champagne. And then it

111

happened! The air raid sirens blasted forth. Drills came anytime, and this was a winner!

"Oh no!" cried the guests, huddling together in the living room.

A buxom vision in pink chiffon, Mom automatically stood tall like a trooper, ready to storm a beachhead. "Lights out immediately!" she ordered, running to a chest of drawers. Mom deftly fumbled through the contents, uncovering a flashlight and armband. From the closet, she pulled her helmet with "WARDEN" across the front and dashed out the door.

She and a neighbor, Mr. Kueglin, were the block wardens and, quite frankly, Dad suspected Mom had a closet hankering for bachelor Kueglin. Mom rather enjoyed patrolling the block together in the dark, searching for violations of the drill manual.

Within 30 minutes or so the "all clear" pierced the night, and our soldier Mom pranced through the door bright-eyed. Off with the armband and helmet, she smoothed the pink chiffon and prepared again to serve the guests.

Dad side-glanced Mom as he uncorked another bottle, mumbling that the war should end soon..not to worry...it's just a brief sacrifice for his country...and he suspects the bachelor's queer anyway.

- Lucille Thompson

Rank Has No Privileges

During World War II, my best friend was stationed in England with the 8th Air Force about 80 miles out of London and relates this incident:

General Jimmy Doolittle was in charge of all operations, visiting airfields before his men left for a mission, showing his support. Casualties were significant; over 10% did not make it back. Morale was decreasing. The crew left each time pondering how many would complete the mission. General Doolittle (who was awarded the Medal of Honor for his raid over Tokyo), was there when they took off and there when they came back.

Returning from a particularly brutal mission 25 thousand feet over Germany, one plane showed a bullet-ridden tail section. General Doolittle rushed to the young tail gunner, who was painfully climbing out and asked, "Son were you in there?"

"Where did you think I was, sir? Out to lunch?"

- Genevieve Kissack

Scarlet Letters

V-J Day! We could hardly believe it. The war was over.
I was Air Force Librarian at Mitchel Field, Long Island, New York. I sailed through the Post Library spreading the news. "I'm going to Times Square on the Long Island Railroad train. If anyone would like to join me, come along."

Four soldiers, three Wafs and 15 members of the French Air Force joined me. None of the Frenchmen could speak English.

Once on the Long Island Railroad, we decided we should identify the members of our group, especially since some had a language problem. Suppose they wandered away from us? A flash of light--lipstick! We could write "V J" on our foreheads.

Oh no! Jean, the young Frenchman riding beside me, had confused Victory over Japan with Victory Day. He had written indelibly on my forehead: "V.D."

Then a soldier saw me. "Wow!" he said. "You'll be the safest woman on Times Square tonight."

- Katherine Kennedy McIntyre

The Sky's the Limit

"Take a card, any card. Look at it. Put it back in the deck."

With those words, a card trick is born. From that moment on, the magician knows exactly where your card is. His objective is to reveal it in the most amazing way possible.

My husband's hobby was magic. In one of his favorite tricks, he would deftly maneuver your chosen card to the top of the deck and daub a sticky substance on the back of it. Pulling another one from the deck, he would triumphantly ask, "Is this your card?"

And you would triumphantly answer, "No!" You felt that *you* had foiled this amateur magician.

After several more fake "Is this your card?" attempts, he would, feigning defeat, hold the deck firmly in his hand, then with an upward thrust, throw it to the ceiling. Splat. Fifty one cards would fall to the floor. Your card would stick to the ceiling, sunny-side-down. Astonished ohs and ahs.

For him, magic was a welcome diversion from the stresses of his work as a writer with the Office of War Information (OWI) during World War II.

When he was asked to entertain at an office party, our living room ceiling became marred with gooey smears, as he practiced that card trick. After all, he would be performing before Elmer Davis, the famous writer and radio commentator appointed director of the OWI by President Roosevelt. Robert Sherwood, already the recipient of his first three Pulitzer Prizes and director of the Overseas Branch of the OWI, would also be there.

The big night arrived. As we entered the ballroom of an elegant old hotel in mid-town Manhattan, our eyes looked up. And up. And up. He was doomed. The ceiling was domed.

- Lucy Almand Harrison

The Sixty Day Wonders

We boasted that it took only sixty days to turn a civilian woman into a Naval Reserve officer, whereas the men had to spend ninety days!

One day, during Midshipmen's School at Smith College in Northampton, Massachusetts, my friend Helen McDaniel and I were walking toward our dorm when I spotted a man in uniform approaching. "Wait," I said, "let me practice my salute." So I walked toward the man, and when we were close enough, I raised my right hand smartly to my forehead in salute. He just stood there with no response. Still holding my hand in salute position, I turned to Helen and asked "Why doesn't he return my salute so I can lower my arm?"

"Because he's not an officer," she said. "He's the mailman."

- Margaret Bates

M-O-N-E-Y Spells Relief

As a Wave during World War II, I was luckier than some, because my Navy job closely followed my social work training. I was placed in the Navy Relief Society office at Miami, Florida, under the chaplain's auspices. Our work largely consisted of helping families of Navy personnel with various problems and providing counseling when needed. We even gave financial assistance to Navy men.

One Saturday, a chaplain was covering the office, when a sailor came in with a long, sad story about his mother who lived in another town and needed immediate cash for a medical problem. The chaplain issued a check, and the sailor went on his way.

On Monday morning, my phone rang. The woman on the line said, "I have a check from your office which is not signed."

"Oh, I'm sorry," I replied. "Just send it to me, and I'll sign it and get it back to you . Where shall I shall I mail it?"

The woman answered innocently, "This is the Hialeah Race Track."

So much for the medical emergency!

- Margaret Bates

A Shirt Tale

As we were moving through the countryside in France, Lt. Kerr of C Battery of my AAA battalion was turning over his laundry to a native mademoiselle. She saw that the tails of his shirts had large notches cut out of them and asked him in French (she could speak no English) what caused the notches.

He explained, in his high school French, that he went to Officer Candidate School as an enlisted man and graduated as an officer. Officers' shirts had epaulets, but enlisted men's did not, so he had pieces cut from the shirt tails to use to make epaulets.

When his laundry returned, his epaulets had all been removed, unstitched, and sewn back into the shirt tails.

- Jim Shearouse

Son of the World War I Leader

On June 5, 1944 (D-Day -1) our First U.S. Army headquarters staff under General Omar Bradley was moving southward toward the marshalling area near Portsmouth, England. There, we were to load onto the ships to lead the attack on the Normandy coast.

Advancing in one great column (a large group, some 200 strong) might have alerted the wrong people to what was going on, so special measures were taken. The MPs broke up the convoy into small groups of about seven vehicles each and directed them down a variety of routes, stopping the units for short lengths of time in odd places. Only the MPs scattered along the way knew the routes and schedules. It certainly gave the rest of us a mighty strange feeling.

Along the way, the unit I was in was pulled off the road and ordered to wait a while on an embankment beside the highway. The man beside me was a fellow staff member. For several months, we had been working together to ready the troops for the Invasion. He was Lieutenant Colonel Francis Pershing, son of General John J. ("Black Jack") Pershing, Commander in Chief of the Allied Expeditionary Forces in World War I.

Disconsolately, Francis said, "This is a heck of a note. When my father was going into France, everyone---especially he--- knew where he was going and when. Here I am going into France, and I don't know where I am or when I'm going to move. I don't know who's ahead of me or who is behind. Oh boy!"

- Jim Shearouse

Spam and Brussels Sprouts

My father's parents, Cyril Granville Smith and Mom Smith, were concerned about their son Vernon being stationed in England and not getting enough greens and meat. They were both convinced that he was going to starve to death. Mom was a doting mother, to say the least, and insisted that once a month a "care" package be sent to her beloved son overseas.

The box, delivered to some destination in Britain near Salisbury, was loaded with canned Spam and Brussels sprouts.

When my Daddy returned from the war, his first announcement was "No Spam or Brussels sprouts."

What my grandparents didn't know was that Brussels sprouts have always been a mainstay vegetable in the British Isles. It's one of their favorite greens. The U.S. Army ate them all during World War II, until they themselves turned green.

Among Daddy's papers brought back from the war was a poem written by one of the men in his company. Daddy's handwritten note at the bottom explains, "To really understand the humor, it would have to be understood that we have been fed Spam until the very word brings groans from us."

Here is the poem:

> At Mail Call here last evening
> A package came for Quinn
> His eagerness overcame him,
> And so he dove right in.

He sorted through the usual things
Which folks from home should send
Toothpaste, razor blades and
Sewing kit with which to mend.

His anticipation rising,
He pushed all these aside
He knew some special item
Under these was sure to hide.

He found the prize - and from his lips
There burst an awful "DAMN!"
For his folks had sent him nothing but
Two lovely cans of SPAM!!!

(The profanity is, of course, deplored,
but is necessary in the interest of
rhyme and trueness to life.)
    Could my father have been "Quinn," the name changed
also in the interest of rhyme? Most likely.

                                    – Joy S. Burton

THEN VS. NOW VS. THE FUTURE

Life's Inevitable Cycle

Each year I'm aware more and more of how much I am endeavoring to grow old gracefully. At the same time, there's a remarkable resemblance to the beginnings of life. For instance:

As a baby, I required a bib at mealtimes. How I wish for one now.

I have begun to limit my conversation to shorter sentences like I did when I was learning to talk; otherwise, I forget what I was going to say.

During an afternoon nap, with head thrown back, mouth dropped open, I awaken to the feel of drool down my chin. But there is no mother to wipe it away.

As a child with growing feet, I had only one or two pairs of shoes at the time. Now I'm down to the same number that comfortably fit my worn-out feet.

I held on to a supporting hand as a little one. Now I welcome a helpful arm when the ground won't stay still.

Like all young children, I said the same thing over and over again until I got what I wanted. Now I do the same thing, only I wait a day or two to repeat it.

When I was little, I had a hard time remembering to do what I had been told. Now, when I go from the kitchen to the bedroom, I forget what my mind sent me in there to do.

As a tyke, I always seemed to have skinned knees and elbows or a scraped chin. Now it's arthritis here, bursitis there, an aching back or shooting pains most anywhere---a new ailment every day.

Growing up, I struggled to gain enough vocabulary to make interesting sentences. Now I have the vocabulary; I just can't think of it when I need it.

In my toddler years, I found getting out of a chair a challenge. It's even more so now.

Time between birthdays and Christmases seemed endless then. Now the weeks go by so fast, it's next week already before I

119

can get through this one.

Mother rocked me to sleep those many years ago, but these days I rock myself to stay awake.

Milk was a necessity for the beginning years. Now it's about all I can drink that doesn't give me indigestion, gas, diarrhea or bloating.

I thought the pages of my storybooks were hard to turn. Now the pages of books, magazines and especially newspapers all seem to be glued together. Takes me twice as long to read the paper every morning.

But I must say that the best thing I have now that I didn't in the beginning years is a zillion warm memories which sustain me through each waking moment. Well, that is, when I can remember them.

- Florine Ledford Olive

Grocery Groans

For most of my life, I've suffered from feelings of inadequacy. But in this day and age of rampant mediocrity, it's becoming more and more difficult to maintain an inferiority complex at any decent level.

The grocery store is a hotbed of incompetence. I've had checkers ring up cabbage as lettuce, rutabagas as sweet potatoes. It's anybody's guess how they interpret such salad greens as endive, romaine or escarole. And heaven help you if you go through the checkout line with a kiwi or artichoke.

The new generation seems unschooled beyond the burger and fries. They unabashedly ask customers the names of even common fruits and vegetables - but not before completing their private conversations with the bagger or the checker in the next lane. Their subjects are predictable: what happened last night, what they'll do tonight, or how much time before they're "out of here."

The thing that bothers me the most is when I appear invisible. I stand hopefully, checkbook in hand, and no one seems able to see me.

It's enough to make me consider trading in my inferiority complex on an identity crisis. Everyone, after all, is entitled to one neurosis.

- Ellen Scarborough

The Chunnel

Call 1-800/EUROSTAR if you wish to realize my perennial childhood dream: a fast train under the English Channel---no more crossings on the choppy waters.

The Chunnel is now open: leave from the center of Paris and arrive in downtown London three hours later.

As a French schoolgirl facing a ride on the ferry to England via the coast of France, I'd fantasize about an underwater subway, when my classmates would watch to determine which one turned green first. It was always I! Or who could look innocent enough after "inadvertently" spraying passengers with a jug of water. It was never I! And then, not getting caught, who could, with one eye, glance luringly (we hoped) at the handsome British skipper, while lowering the other eye in silent prayer with our chaperone. I lost on that as well! What jolly ole times we had on the slow-paced ferry under summer skies---and now, with this monster at speeds of up to 200 miles per hour, what are students to do for fun?

The French are right: "Beware of what you wish for---it may be granted."

- Genevieve Kissack

Charlotte's a Zoo

I can tell y'all that Charlotte, North Carolina, is on the map now! We may not have a city zoo, but exotic animals abound, and because of them, our fair village has hit the "big time."

In earlier times, buffalo roamed along local creek banks, rabbits scampered from field to field and rattlers slithered through dense woods. Indian hunters and gatherers and early white settlers found food plentiful. When General Cornwallis came through this area during the American Revolution, our people pestered his men with so many ambushes that he called this "a hornet's nest of rebellion."

As of 1995, we have a coliseum for Hornets, a football stadium for Panthers and a large baseball field for Homer the Dragon's Charlotte Knights.

During the Great Depression and World War, when the residents of our green-treed town were still "bubbas," they were indeed fortunate whenever they found beef steaks, chicken legs, and pork butts in neighborhood grocery stores.

121

But now, we can visit an upscale supermarket built to resemble Monticello, where we can purchase fresh buffalo, rabbit and rattlesnake.

Have we progressed---or regressed?

- Joy Smith Burton

Will Mary Ann Be a
Thrifty Eccentric, Too?

Those in my closest circles know me as thrifty. Or creatively clever in saving a dime. Or gifted in grappling with a budget.

The trait pops up often---as when my daughter Charlene, her friend Kay and I looked at pre-cut quilt pieces in a craft shop. "Mama, do you want one of these kits?" asked Charlene.

"Buy quilt pieces?" I inquired, indignant. "You're supposed to make quilts from scraps of cloth you would otherwise throw away. That yellow quilt on your bed, made by my grandmother, has fabric from dresses I wore as a child. Floral pieces in that quilt are from pajamas I made when I took sewing in the eighth grade. The whole point in crafts is to use your leftovers."

Charlene explained to Kay, "Mama makes pillowcases from the corners of old sheets worn out in the middle."

"Really?" said Kay, impressed.

"She made a beautiful velveteen pillow," Charlene continued, "from pants I outgrew. She used trimming from an old pair of drapes. Mama was a Depression kid, and she never throws away anything."

"But we don't have a sewing machine," said Kay.

"Mama would say that's what fingers are for."

My children, overlooking my oddities, try to be helpful. While preparing for his spring yard work, my son-in-law Tim said to me, "I'm ordering pine needles. Do you want me to get you a couple of bales?"

"No, thank you," I said. "I don't use them. Most people rake up the leaves and grass cuttings, bag them and throw them away. Then they put pine needles for mulch. I take the economical way and rake the grass and leaves into the shrubbery and flower beds. It makes terrific mulch and fertilizer."

"I've found a good plumber," said Tim. "You said the commode in your bathroom was acting up. Do you want him to look at it?"

"Not anymore. I fixed it with a twist'em that came with the garbage bags."

"You sure you don't need a plumber?" asked Tim.

"No," I said, "the toilet works just fine."

My children don't hesitate to discuss my savings eccentricities in my presence. At a family dinner, Charlene said to my son, Russ, "The oddest thing Mama does is tell how wonderful the miracle drugs like penicillin are, how people used to stay sick a long time and maybe died. But she never takes an antibiotic herself, because she says it costs too much. 'Besides,' she says, 'the body heals itself.' Mama has weird ideas."

"It's not that her ideas are all that weird," said my son. "It's just that she's got so many of them. Have you ever seen her run the plastic throw-away picnic cups through the dishwasher?"

"Or," added my daughter-in-law, "watched her pinch the teeniest bits of chicken off the bones to make salad?"

"She uses the backs of my old homework papers to do her writing," said my grandson Stephen.

"And when I grow up," said my granddaughter Mary Ann, "I'm going to be just like Grandma. I'm going to pull the brown envelopes out of Dad's trash can, and I'm going to eat all my meals at Wendy's!"

- Frances Eppley

What's a Body to Do?

Sometime in the 1940s, I strolled in from school and overheard my mom's bridge club discussing the neighbor who had brazenly decided to jazz herself up and color her hair. It looked like a "lady-of-the-evening red," they buzzed. In those days, coloring one's hair, especially red, seemed to be a scandalous act, if you weren't some type of performer or in the public eye most of the time.

Wow! Have we come a long way Baby! Today, anything goes, and red is mild compared to fried, dyed, frizzled, wet look, dry look, androgenous back flips and front dips, and dreadlocks in all colors. Even hair clipped to a quarter inch has artistically shaved-in designs of butterflies, sculls, lover's names or favorite sports teams.

Moving a tad down to the ears, I remember the bridge ladies' comment about an Italian mom piercing her new baby's ears. "Foreigners!" they scowled. "You never know what to expect from them."

Now girls do it, boys do it, and even some ol' grannies do it--holes everywhere! Three or four in both ears, eyelids, nose, tongues and places we could only chuckle about. Ouch! If you could shake that body upside down, surely it would leak.

Worse yet, the entire anatomy has become an artist's canvas. One tattoo, years ago, and you were certainly headed down the halls of degradation.

The other day at church, I spotted a sedate young woman, and there peeking over her back neckline was a long-lashed eye. As I moved, it appeared to follow. Wrists, arms, ankles, fronts, rears are laced with color. Once saved for the boxer, biker or hitchhiker, tattoos are here to stay---indelibly.

Let's face it folks, decorating is "in"! I wonder if the bridge ladies' motto, "She's such a plain Jane" will ever apply again.

- Lucille Thompson

The Generation Gap

My dear grandchildren,

Based on the way things are going, by the time you are grown, your world is going to be the cat's pajamas (that's good). Take for example:

You will have to take out a second mortgage on your house to buy your kids a pair of name-brand athletic shoes. But you'll save a lot of money on bathing suits - a Bandaid will do the trick.

Deciding on the best politician for the job at election time will be easy. Just vote for the one who has been involved in the most affairs.

Fast food chains will be non-existent, because they brewed their coffee too hot.

Schools will add courses to their curricula in what a baseball game is, latest sightings of Elvis and in how to date in an upright position.

Movies will have become passe, because writers and producers could no longer come up with something new that takes place in the bedroom.

About the time you will be graduating from college, O.J. Simpson's trials and appeals could be winding down.

When the verdict is in, maybe the country will get back to normal trashing the incumbent administration, watching soaps again and worrying about the spotted owl.

English will be the universal language, except for teenagers, who will still have a language all their own.

Doctors will again be making house calls because they'll be so specialized they won't have enough patients to afford office space.

With more and more money being spent on designer apparel, fancy foods and toys for your family pets, you will be able to claim Fido and Socks as deductions on your income tax.

There will be support groups throughout the country for those addicted to filing lawsuits.

The generation you tabbed "old folks" will be the majority age group running the country and singing "Happy days are here again!"

Immigrants will be allowed to enter the country only if they agree not to open a restaurant.

The legislators who worked so hard to change Medicare and Social Security will be into retirement age and wishing they had kept their mouths shut.

Most everything will be unisex - clothes, hair styles and sports teams. But dating surely will be uninteresting.

Instead of a chicken in every pot, there'll be a cellular phone in every pocket.

The two predominant political parties will be known as Forked Tongues and the Jackasses. We're not too far from that now.

Pop singers will once again perform without twitching and jumping about as if they were possessed.

Sports events will have become so violent that even the spectators will have to wear helmets.

An optional feature on your electrically operated car will be rotor blades for instant conversion from road to air travel - a boon to compulsive lane-changers.

But I'm not going to worry about you. I am confident you'll survive. And if you make mistakes, don't fret - just write a book about it.

> Lovingly,
> Your devoted grandmother
> Florine Ledford Olive

GIVE YOUR FAVORITE "SEASONED" CITIZEN
A LITTLE NOSTALGIA AND LOTS O' CHUCKLES

A. Borough Books specializes in books by and for the 50+ generation

To order - Complete this form and mail to:
A. Borough Books   P.O. Box 15391
Charlotte NC 28211

20%
discount for
10 or more

_____copies *Gray-Haired Grins & Giggles*
Guess what - Grandy & Grammy have a sense of humor, too!
True tales from 45 authors   Paperback @ $12.95 $_____

_____copies *World War II: It Changed Us Forever*
From the battlefront to the homefront and places in between
33 authors tell it like it was! Paperback @ $12.95 $_____

_____copies *Only Forty Miles of Pavement*
Tales of a traveling salesman from oil boom days
through the Depression   Hardback @ $16.95 $_____

_____copies *Prohibition Didn't End in '33*
How "wets" got their liquor in a "dry" nation, state
or county   Paperback @ $10.95 $_____

Shipping & handling $2 up to 5 books; $4 up to 10 $_____

NC residents add 6% tax (78¢, 78¢, $1.02 or 66¢ each) $ _____

TOTAL $ _____

Please make check or money order to A. Borough Books

Name_____

Address_____

City,   State,   Zip_____

Phone   #_____

If this is a library copy, please photocopy this form.